DREAM BIG:

AND AWAKEN TO
YOUR POSSIBILITIES

DR. D. A. FLANAGAN, DNP, CRNA

Chasing Dreams Forever,

#DREAMBIG

SPS
SELF-PUBLISHING SERVICES LLC
HELPING YOU WITH ALL YOUR PUBLISHING NEEDS

a memoir

HOW A CERTIFIED REGISTERED NURSE ANESTHETIST
DISCOVERED A CALLING IN HIS CAREER

DREAM
big

DR. D. A. FLANAGAN, DNP, CRNA

Dream Big:
KDP ebook: 978-1-7345918-1-1
Draft2Digital ebook: 978-1-7345918-4-2
KDP print book: 978-1-7345918-0-4

Dream Big Road Map:
KDP ebook: 978-1-7345918-2-8
Draft2Digital ebook: 978-1-7345918-5-9

Dream Big & Road Map (Combo):
KDP ebook: 978-1-7345918-3-5
Draft2Digital ebook: 978-1-7345918-6-6

Edited by Self Publishing Services
Cover Design by Meld Media
Formatting by Meld Media

CONTENTS

DEDICATION

To the women who, together, raised a truly unique man by pooling every resource they could muster to make dreams come true. Especially you, "Ba-Ba."

I love each and every one of you!

PREFACE

As a black, male, and board-certified registered nurse anesthetist (CRNA), I have been highlighted in various university magazines, newspaper write-ups, and on-camera interviews. By the age of twenty-five, I had been placed on a pedestal.

I naively thought I would be uplifted and exhilarated by all that acclaim. In reality, my platform felt more like an island of isolation. I felt lonely as a prodigy within my profession. Not loneliness in the traditional definition of the word. But more so in the sense of being unique because there was no one around who looked or acted like me.

I was born in the Deep South, a region of the US still trying to rectify and remember its past while simultaneously struggling to embrace the ever-diverse landscape of the twenty-first century. Poverty, racism, and crime were common themes in the immediate world around me. Today, my hometown, Chattanooga, Tennessee, is a tourist destination with new high-rise condos and boutique restaurants. But in the 1980s and 1990s when I was growing up, the landscape was much different for black families like mine, who, for generations, had been banished to one side of the tracks.

Somehow, I found myself a CRNA with a doctoral degree from Columbia University before the age of forty. I'm a black man, and I'm not dead or in jail as the statistics told me all my life I would be. I believe it's because I chose to "Dream Big!"

I gambled on myself and beat the odds. That is the story this book tells.

My story is not a stand-alone occurrence, but it also is not a common one. I feel that it is important for me to share my experiences so that those who want to follow a path similar to mine know what to expect. For progress to be made, I believe we must share both the thrills and tribulations we faced on our way to success.

In a world dominated by entertainment-based public figures, I believe sharing my story will help inspire other black teenage boys and young adults, as well as any person of color who needs encouragement when they feel their back's against the wall. We all have greatness in us. It is rooted in our DNA through our ancestors.

For the past five years, I have worked on this book, revisiting and confronting all the experiences that shaped me. There were lows and highs I had either forgotten or suppressed. Framing each of those moments within the educational achievements that have instinctively become plot points on the road map of my journey has been not only therapeutic but also exhausting. I find solace in knowing that this story can be a turning point for others, even if just for one person.

Welcome to my story. Enjoy this rollercoaster of pain, excitement, and perseverance.

CHAPTER 1:
THE BLENDED FAMILY THEORY

"Family is everything. I'm talking about everything. The way we were brought up is family first, no matter what. My mom was caring and nurturing. She always told us to stay close. So from the beginning of the generation, that's all we knew. If you ain't got something and I got it, you can have it. I'll get something else. Even if you are not family. If we know you need something, our family will pull together and help you. We always try to look out for the next person, regardless of what color they are or whether they are grown, children, or whatever. That's the type of family we are." – Deborah Odom

I've been equipped by imperfection to exist outside of and to advocate against norms. My childhood was homogenous in that my perspective was restricted to my neighborhood. From family to friends, the social frameworks I was exposed to were just like my own. I did not know what a nuclear family was. I was not introduced to the concept of one dad, one mom, and two-and-a-half kids until I was a teenager. I came to learn that my mom, aunts, uncles, cousins, and half brothers who occasionally lived under the same roof made up what is defined as a blended family. By the time I found that out, my ties to family were rooted deep. A dynasty-like pride outweighed any self-pity.

At 7:47 a.m. on June 18, 1984, two twenty-year-olds, Deborah Odom and Victor Flanagan, Sr., welcomed their 7.8-pound son in Erlanger Hospital of Chattanooga, Tennessee. One could argue my mom gave birth to twins. Born under the Gemini zodiac sign, I have always felt my life was two-sided. There is the double consciousness that comes with being black. There is the street code that comes with being lower income but wanting the American Dream without abandoning your 'hood. And there is the two-edged sword of exposure that leaves you constantly at war with practicality versus pleasure. I'm speaking in twos, but my parents' union ended not long after I was born. My mom became a unit of one: a single parent.

My mom is the offspring of a divorced mother. She was born on March 7, 1963, and her mother, Wilma "Ba-Ba" Daniels, endured physical and emotional abuse from her father, James "Bubba" Henry Odom, Sr., who was an alcoholic. My mom's first example of lasting love did not come until her mother's second marriage, to Howard Daniels. The same year she had me, she went on to earn her nursing assistant certificate. And not too long afterward, my sister, Dominique Flanagan, was born on October 13, 1986. The two of us did not save my parents' union, though. They went their separate ways, and my mom poured herself into being a strong, independent provider and protector. She went on to attend Edmondson Junior College, where she later received her associate's degree in computer science. For twenty-five years, she built a career as an insurance claims adjuster.

Also, like her mother, my mom found romantic longevity the second time around when she married my stepfather, Arthur Tibbs, in 1990.

As I became a teenager, old enough to comprehend the real world, she taught me the value of hard work. I saw that her pride, determination, work ethic, and nurturing spirit would not allow her to receive food stamps or government assistance. She had grown up in the housing projects of Chattanooga, and she refused to allow her children to endure that. My mother is known for having a stoic attitude and for being very rigid in her approach to values and confrontations. Even though she's the middle child of three, she is often labeled the mean sibling. I believe it's all rooted in a deeper determination not to be taken advantage of. She is a product of the hustles and swindles of the inner city and of a household of domestic violence. Protection is her lived experience. Her smiles and jokes are the armor she wears.

Like my mom, my dad is also the product of a step-in father, Ernest Lee Watley, Jr., and a remarried mother, Mary Patterson Adams. My dad's father, Montrell Flanagan, abandoned his mother shortly after he was born. My dad married and divorced, and gave me half brothers and half sisters along the way: Victor Antonio Flanagan, Jr., Tyler Antonio Flanagan, and Amber Victoria Flanagan.

Born August 16, 1963, my dad is my grandmother's only child. A charismatic free spirit, my grandmother opened life's doors and let him explore. At the same time, she instilled in him the values of work and independence. My dad roamed Chattanooga, gaining friends from all corners and playing every sport he could sign up for. I believe the abandonment of his father and a series of other unfortunate encounters with family left a void he tried to fill. Outside of his unyielding dedication to my grandmother, for him, family was fleeting. He has always connected more deeply with the friends he's met along the way.

Yet he did seek strong, powerful black men he could aspire to be like, most notably Malcolm X. He connected with the belief of defending what's yours by any means necessary. The freedom my grandmother allowed him fueled his independent thinking and entrepreneurial spirit. He could go from fishing to building tree houses to investigating car engines to being lectured by teachers. Eventually, when I was in high school, he graduated from the University of Tennessee at Chattanooga with a bachelor's degree in engineering. He went on to earn his master's degree in engineering and another master's in business administration.

I believe the common threads connecting my mom and dad were drive, determination, and that caretaker spirit. These traits manifest in different ways, but they are the foundation of their lives and my upbringing.

I grew up in Hamilton County, where, according to the *1990 Tennessee Census Report*, the population was around 200,000. The makeup was about 80 percent white, 19 percent black, and 1 percent Asian or other ethnic descent, according to the *1990 Tennessee Census Report*. I lived in the valley of the city, noted for the Civil War battlefield of Missionary Ridge. This majority-black area saw its fair share of drugs, crime, gangs, and violence. My heads of household included my mother and her siblings and their spouses: Aunt Tresa Odom-Stripling, Uncle Kenneth Stripling, Uncle James Odom, Jr., and Aunt Josephine Odom. And, with them came my earliest best friends, my cousins: Tia Wordlaw, Turnae Watson, James Odom, III, and Jamie Odom.

For most black families in inner-city Chattanooga, my household arrangement was standard, and it had been for generations. Mothers, grandmothers, sisters, and cousins showed support in every way necessary for survival.

CHAPTER 2:

HOWARD HIGH SCHOOL

"One thing that Donté does well is listen. He still listens today when I give him advice. I introduced critical thinking to him when he was ten years old. He has used this type of thinking to become the man he is today, taking from that technique to come to sound decisions." – Victor A. Flanagan, my dad

As in many Southern cities where the black community is the minority, the communication grapevine is thorough. If you want to know about or meet a person, just work your way through your family until you find the common denominator in theirs. For my family, Howard High School was the shared resource.

In the 1950s and 1960s, a vast majority of black Chattanooga residents attended Howard High. Centrally located to the projects, it was easy for students to walk to school, thus keeping them out of the sight of the larger white community. The ironic result is that the school became an ecosystem of black empowerment and civil rights activism. Howard, now The Howard School, still stands and now serves a student population that is largely black and Hispanic. The projects are still there, too; they're now called Mary Walker Towers, a 160-unit affordable housing community.

My family might not fit into the white-picket-fence stereotype, but there are elements of our storyline—like high school rivalry—that trigger an Americana type of nostalgia. My parents were the epitome of small-town sweethearts. My dad was a mover and shaker in Chattanooga. The discipline of his step-in father, Ernest Watley, was his saving grace for staying in line. Granddaddy Watley, as I call him, was a community leader and activist. After serving his country in World

War II, he came home and demanded that the same freedoms he had been afforded as a soldier be granted to him as an American citizen. The Urban League of Greater Chattanooga served as Granddaddy Watley's platform for change. He was a voice and a fighter for the black community, helping expand and secure job opportunities for black residents for forty years until his passing in 2013.

In the early 1970s, Granddaddy Watley secured one of the first black-owned nightclubs in the city. He named the club Johari, which is the Swahili word for jewel. The club became a nightly meeting place for black men and women across the Tennessee Valley, offering a safe and entertaining space for patrons and steady employment for residents. On Johari's "Blue Mondays," patrons could enjoy the fixed-price special of steak and potatoes. Patrons ranged from national talents, like the Ohio Players, to local performers who competed for trophies and monetary prizes. It was in Johari that my dad discovered and honed his knack for nightlife and entertainment.

Granddaddy Watley started hosting young adult nights, which gave my dad a more integral role in the club's operations. My dad started hosting his own talent shows, which he eventually deejayed as well. Through his work as a DJ, he became immersed in the city's entertainment scene, learning the ins and outs of the music and concert industries. He made a name for himself in the community. So much so that my mom caught word of him.

My dad strayed from his family's Howard roots, attending Kirkman High School across the historical dividing line of the city now known as MLK Boulevard. MLK Boulevard was previously known as 9th Street. In the '40s, '50s, and '60s, it was the unspoken border that divided the black side of the city from the white. My mom, on the other hand, stayed true as a second-generation Howard Tiger. My parents had actually attended middle school together at Alton Park, and my dad admits he had eyes for her even then. But, because they went to high schools on different sides of town, their paths didn't connect again until afterward. My dad went out of his way to stay connected. The son of a single mother who promoted his development of self-reliance, my dad spent the majority of his time working various jobs starting as early as twelve years old. Because of this, he was able to purchase his first car in tenth grade, which was much sooner than his peers. Through a random encounter, my dad learned my mom lived on Glenwood Drive. From then on, when he was en route to school, he would go out of his way to drive by my mom's house to see her standing by the bus stop, blow his horn, and wave at her. But he never stopped for a full conversation. This continued for a couple of years until eventually my mother recognized who he was. Then, on one fateful evening at the Johari, they finally struck up a conversation.

My mom was at the club with her older sister, my aunt Tresa. Back in the day, they called my aunt "Big-O" as she was not only the oldest sibling of the Odom kids but also the tallest until the growth spurts of adolescence. On this night, Big-O had a song she wanted to hear, and she didn't know how to make it happen. After my aunt mentioned it a time or two, my mom finally explained to her that she knew the DJ, my dad. My mom went over to the DJ booth and asked my dad to play "Cool" by The Time. Right there, he had his opportunity. They exchanged phone numbers, and, later that week, after he confirmed with her that a date wouldn't be too serious, he persuaded her to go to Steak and Ale with him. My dad knew Steak and Ale, now Bennigan's, well because this was also one of the places he worked part-time as a busboy. After that date, my parents built a friendship and a relationship. From teaching her to drive his manual-shift car to trips to Atlanta, he and she were inseparable. Young and in love.

Similarly, my grandparents also fell in love young, as high school sweethearts. At the aforementioned Howard High, my dad's mom was a classmate of my mom's mom and my aunt. My dad's dad also had Tiger pride but graduated in a different class. Age didn't keep the two sweethearts separated, however. I've heard stories of my grandparents' teenage love affair, including locker-time hand-holding and gym class jealousy meltdowns. Apparently, the two were quite popular. My grandfather was the chocolate young man known for his charm. Dark complexions have historically been a thing among the Flanagans, but my grandmother apparently threw off my odds; my complexion is more comparable to caramel. My grandmother was the fair-skinned girl with long, wavy hair who kept her nose in books. One year, my grandparents were even awarded the yearbook superlative of "best smile." But beneath the surface, their bond was really responsibility, as they both held jobs to help their parents make ends meet. So, when they discovered they were having a child, everyone assumed things would be taken care of. The predictions were wrong, though. My grandparents' love story was cut short just like my parents'.

My grandfather left town to find his way in the world after my dad was born. The notion of hard work was not what my grandmother was unprepared for; it was the heartbreak. She never had another child after my dad. My grandfather eventually made his way to Rochester, New York, where he married and had kids. My grandmother worked multiple jobs until she landed at Chattanooga's DuPont plant. She ended up working there for more than thirty years, moving up to managerial positions and eventually moving around the East Coast from Delaware to Maryland before returning to Chattanooga, where she lives now. All of those years, she raised my dad as best she could, aiming to make sure he had everything he needed and never felt his father's absence financially. But my grandfather's absence was felt by my dad, both physically and emotionally. It was felt by my entire family, in fact.

The Flanagans still have a presence in Chattanooga. But my grandmother and dad have had little contact with them. I have had no relationship with my paternal grandfather and little interaction with his side of the family. For me, they are estranged. My dad has reimagined what it means to be a Flanagan man for my half brothers and me. And much of that is due to Granddaddy Watley.

CHAPTER 3:
THE ERNEST WATLEY
SCHOOL OF THOUGHT

"Donté is a sweet person. He's got his head on straight. He knows what he wants to do with his life. He's a good man. Donté had a lot of respect for Ernest. I never saw Donté give Ernest any problems at all. I'm sure if Ernest was alive, he would be so proud of Donté and him doing all the things that he is supposed to do to make life better." – Maria Watley, wife of my late step-grandfather

Granddaddy Watley came into my dad's life when he was ten years old. He officially married my grandmother in 1977. Granddaddy Watley's life experiences became wisdom he eventually imparted to my dad, my half brothers, and me as life lessons.

One particular experience with Granddaddy Watley taught me about compassion. Every few months, he would host afternoon lunches and sometimes dinners at Johari and call them "Appreciation Nights." I remember going with him one time as a young boy. On the way, he explained to me the importance of taking care of those who take care of you. When we arrived, he pointed out one of his loyal customers, Mr. Robinson.

"He comes in here nearly every week and supports the business. He's struggling with health problems within his family and with a dying mother. And yet, he still comes out with a smile and takes these moments to recharge and step out of his present reality," Granddaddy Watley explained.

Sharing those meals with his customers was his way of saying thank you and showing them he was a part of their lives. I saw just how much the community respected Granddaddy Watley because he treated everyone with respect and dignity. He taught me to never turn my back on my community, especially those who are taking their time and money to support you. Granddaddy Watley lived this way his entire life, even after he underwent leg amputations.

He called me one day, when I happened to be in town, and asked me to drive him around town for a couple of errands. I had no idea what to expect, but I agreed. He had a specialized van that was outfitted to allow him to drive using handheld devices on the steering wheel and special gears for the gas and brakes. He drove across the city, giving me directions at each place we stopped. It was like his own personal community outreach campaign as we visited his friends and former colleagues and customers. Many of these people were too ill to leave their own homes or simply didn't have the financial means. Every door we knocked on, these elderly people lit up with joy at the sight of Granddaddy Watley and the opportunity to catch up on each other's families and lives. I was amazed that he went through so much effort to stay connected to his community.

On our way home, Granddaddy Watley said, "Donté, never get too busy or too important that you forget the lives you've met along the way."

I realized that experience was his way of showing me that even after the business closes, those relationships live on. No matter one's station in life, no one wants to be forgotten. Looking back on everything I learned from Granddaddy Watley, four themes always seemed to repeat: loyalty, honor, humility, and generosity. Granddaddy Watley defined loyalty as keeping your word even when the consequences may not be in your favor. For him, loyalty was the foundation of trust. He told me about friendships and business partnerships that he walked away from because someone proved disloyal. It was the one thing he said he would not forgive. I learned that loyalty is a mark of one's ability to show respect to themselves and to others. Either you are able to or you are not.

Granddaddy Watley said true honor is putting another person ahead of you. In business, he learned that honor was the foundation of winning over customers and stakeholders. His true edge was in his ability to win over people of all ages, races, and backgrounds. The trick, he told me, is to be definitive without being disrespectful. Everyone has an angle. It's your job to find out what that angle is and meet them on a common ground. And it's easier to do if you're charming. Granddaddy Watley said if you can make someone smile, you've got them hooked. Granddaddy Watley knew that humility is like a thread; it holds everything together. He taught me that we all have been constructed of an imperfect cloth, and, at any moment, the things afforded to us can be instantly taken away. Every decision you make on the continuum of life is one that can shape your future. He showed me that anyone can show respect when they are in the position of inferiority, but only the humble can give respect when they are in the position of authority.

Generosity is a trait Granddaddy Watley drilled into my dad, and he, as result, emphasized it with me. Granddaddy Watley believed that generosity should be rooted in self-motivation. He was not an enabler or someone who gave handouts. He gave because it was his choice. Granddaddy Watley was known for giving black men, specifically, jobs at his business and at those of his closest friends. He did not award and walk away. He and his friends monitored those employees' characters. Every loan or act of kindness came with an expectation and obligation. If it was not met, the bridge was burned.

Shared knowledge was important to Granddaddy Watley; I saw that in the way he passed along lessons to my dad and me. When I was young, my dad told me about a man named Craftsman. He was one of Granddaddy Watley's colleagues at the Johari who was responsible for booking acts and talent. At his day job, he was a vice president at the local bank, First Tennessee. One day at the club, when my dad was just eighteen years old, Craftsman asked my dad if he had any credit. My dad had no idea what that meant, and he didn't understand the benefits or pitfalls that came with it. Craftsman told my dad to meet him at the bank. The following week they met, and Craftsman took the time to not only educate my dad on the perils of credit but also explain the leverage that comes with having good credit. My dad left that meeting with his first line of credit, which helped him fund his early entrepreneurial endeavors as a DJ and concert promoter. A year later, Craftsman died of a heart attack. That story made Granddaddy Watley's lesson of "each one, teach one" stick with me. I understood the urgency to share information, teach, and give back.

Granddaddy Watley once said, "I'm in a privileged position, but how can our community improve if I fail to share these experiences and opportunities with those who are less fortunate than me? As you learn, never be selfish in your knowledge. Share it so each of us may have an opportunity to grow and flourish."

Granddaddy Watley, while a teacher, was also a human, flawed. Life in the nightclub introduced him to a lot of slick talkers and pretty faces, one of whom was Marie Watley, who he later married. My grandmother, who had helped build that nightclub, often cooking menu items herself, eventually remarried a final time. But she never forced her son to walk away from that bond. And Granddaddy Watley remained as my dad's step-in father and my grandfather.

Granddaddy Watley shaped much of my value system, while my experiences at the black, Christian church influenced my moral code. Because I grew up in a Southern black household, religion was a major part of my life. My family attended Antioch Primitive Baptist Church, a small community church strategically placed discretely inside Chattanooga's all-black neighborhood of Orchard Knob. The neighborhood continues to be predominantly black, and the church continues to be a refuge for members of the community who may be suffering the struggles of poverty or inner-city neglect. As a child, my mother, who was not a regular at church, would send me with my aunt Jean or Granny Wilma. I spent at least two days a week at church, oftentimes active in Sunday school and morning service in addition to evening service. When I was old enough to carry a tune, I was also enrolled in the children's choir and went to practice reluctantly every week. Then there was also midweek Bible study. As I entered my teenage years, my mother began to take a more active role in my religious experiences when she became a member at Olivet Baptist Church. It had a new, more modern, and younger congregation, and that experience gave me a broader array of friends within the church.

My dad would take me to church from time to time. But he did not hold the same reverence for religious institutions as my mom's side of the family did. He felt there was too much poverty and too many failures to deliver assistance and develop the community to rely on man's religious institutions. He saw the church as a business that did not give back to its patrons. Additionally, his admiration for Malcolm X and the Nation of Islam led him to see it as more productive, with its belief in a higher being and expectation for self-governance.

My spiritual leanings are a blend of my religious experiences with both of my parents. I classify myself as a Christian, but I am a staunch critic of the institution of the modern church. Having grown up in the conservative setting of the Baptist church, I have a difficult time blending the secular world with that of the traditional church. I've long believed that each person has their own personal relationship with God. I believe that pastors, teachers, and leaders within the church are placed in positions to assist with the interpretations of text. But I also believe that walking with God is a very personal journey. With that said, I do believe that God has given us the free will to walk this Earth and deal with the scenarios and dilemmas that present themselves. I believe that when making every good and bad decision, there is a moment, a definitive moment in time, where we must choose our destiny, and those encounters are not by chance.

God does not and will not put more on our plates than we can handle. At every turn, we have been groomed to deal with whatever obstacle stands in our way. Each of us has our journey, but it's up to us to have faith that God has already equipped us with what we need to get through the journey. This belief has always given me a sense of calm when adversity arises and encourages me to meet every opportunity as a learning experience. I'm drawn to spirituality, and that leads me to make decisions based on magnetic or repulsive feelings. Spirituality ultimately has allowed me to look at what I have faced and what I will face with positivity.

CHAPTER 4:
WOODMORE ELEMENTARY

"With me being at the rec center, we talked on a different level, not so much as aunt and nephew but as me being the director and him being a participant. There were some kids that were special, and not in that rowdy, ghetto bunch versus church-going kids. I didn't say Donté couldn't play with them, but he couldn't be buddies with them. Uh-uh. He blended in with everybody else. He just was exceptional in terms of education. He wasn't going to let anything stand in the way of what he wanted to do. And he and I discussed stuff like that. I don't care what it is, if that's what you want to do, just go for it. Nothing beats a failure but a try." – Jackie Simpson, my great-aunt

The summer between my second and third grade, my mother decided it would be best for us to move into our own house, away from the family house on Glenwood Drive. We moved into a duplex home that we shared with my mother's best friend and her daughter on one side of the duplex and my mother, her then fiancé, and my sister on the other side. Because of the relocation, we were rezoned for a new elementary school, full of new dilemmas and experiences. Woodmore Elementary was where I forged some of my fondest childhood memories as I began to navigate a new community as an outsider, but not before a few missteps along the way—beginning with my introduction to martial arts.

Sports were my first avenue for asserting myself, especially my favorite: basketball. My aunt Jackie, my maternal grandmother's sister Jacqueline, was the director at a local parks and recreation center, so I was able to try an array of sports. I went on to win in citywide tournaments. It was actually sports that shaped me to be a competitor in everything I undertake. Many of the competitive characteristics I gained were nurtured by watching my dad and my brother, Victor, Jr., who viewed competition as only winning or losing. Maybe it was not the most conventional parenting model, but it motivated me to achieve and taught me useful life skills. It gave me a leg up by not allowing me to make excuses and allowing me to experience failure and learn how to recover from it with hard work. Playing sports also showed me the benefits of teamwork and leadership; my dad stressed to me that people should be able to depend on leaders to deliver any time they are called upon.

Before I fell in love with basketball during the era of the GOAT (greatest of all time) Michael Jordan, I experimented with Tae Kwon Do. My father was a skilled fighter and had participated in fighting matches with minimal coverage from protective gear. So, of course, as soon as it was physically possible, I enrolled in a similar sport. I was this pigmy of a being, kicking and punching wood planks and doing push-ups and flips under the guidance of Chattanooga's infamous Mr. Hanner. I was advancing through all the stages of the program on my way to being a black belt until something very predictable happened; I started practicing those striking techniques on my peers at preschool. Unprovoked or provoked, it didn't matter. I was the little shit: energetic, unoccupied, and bored. After the administration called my mother about my senseless and unacceptable behavior, she put an end to the martial arts experiment altogether after giving me her own rendition of Tae Kwon Do.

I never hit anyone again...unprovoked. Because I did not want to provoke the wrath of my mother any more than necessary, I remained very cautious about my physical altercations after the cessation of my Tae Kwon Do lessons.

Something, however, caused a brief lapse in judgment a couple years later. During my third year at Woodmore Elementary School, one event gave me more insight into life than I could have imagined as an eight-year-old. I was with friends on the playground during recess, one of whom happened to be Shauntae Boston. Shauntae was sweet, fun, and lively, just like me. I was a talker in class and at times wreaked havoc on teachers because I would disturb other students after I finished my assignments. Well, Shauntae was a classmate who I would often talk to because she finished her work in a timely fashion as well. We would joke about the teacher or other friends in the school or whatever songs were popular at the time.

But something went terribly wrong with our communication on the playground that one afternoon. Somewhere between a friendly game of tag and running around the playground, Shauntae and I had an encounter that resulted in some shoving back and forth. Eventually, she punched me in my chest a time or two. By natural instinct, I pulled my arm back, swung at her face, and connected. I don't know if it was her immediate screaming and crying while she grabbed and covered her eye or something deeper within myself, but I instantly knew I had done a terrible, unforgivable thing. What followed was an unforgettable introduction to what has come to be known as corporal punishment. I was marched down to the principal's office, but he wasn't there that afternoon. That was far from the end of that encounter. I was forced to stay in the principal's office the remainder of the day until my mom picked me up from school. She didn't even bother to lecture me. She simply said, "You know you're in trouble when you get home."

I knew a whipping would ensue as soon as we got to the house. Hours after the hands-on lesson delivered by my mom, which, ironically, I did not consider corporal punishment, it was my dad's turn to weigh in on the matter. What followed was a sit-down father-son lecture that taught me from that day forward to never lay a harmful hand on a woman in any manner. He asked how I would I feel if someone did any harm to my mom, grandmothers, or sisters. He went on to express how wonderfully made women are and how God placed men on Earth to protect and honor them, not hit or abuse them. I thought this was the end of my discipline, as I was sure to never forget those reactions or those lectures.

But it didn't end there.

A week later, Principal Lott returned. He was immediately updated on the goings-on of the week. By this point, I was back in the classroom and reconciled with Shauntae after apologies and playful games. What did we hear? Both of our names were called over the school intercom as we were summoned to the principal's office. In the office, Principal Lott, known for being hard-nosed and an enforcer, met us, ready to rectify the situation on his own terms. He asked us both what had happened, and we both recounted our stories.

After, he asked Shauntae, "How long did you have a black eye?"

She responded, "About three days."

He said, "Okay."

Shauntae was dismissed, but not me. I sat there all alone, eye to eye with the figure every kid in the school knew could inflict the most memorable of swings on a behind.

He said to me, "Shauntae had to endure three days of a black eye, and now you get to endure these three licks. Let them be a reminder to never raise your hand to a woman again."

That was the first of two paddlings I'd receive at the hand of Principal Lott. The other was for throwing rocks on the playground after I had already been placed in timeout for talking. I probably deserved many more.

This was my upbringing as a black child in the 1990s. My world was unapologetically black, and it demanded respect and discipline. If children misbehaved at school, they were disciplined at school and at home. Any misbehavior could be punished by any witness within reach. We were expected to mind our elders, meaning any adult, and we were expected to try our hardest and achieve in every activity.

There was no escaping the rules because there was no escaping family. I grew up in the "family house" as we called it, and there were six to twelve children and adults living in our two-bedroom, two-bathroom home at any given time. We gathered together and fellowshipped all the time. Because of that, I've always been comfortable in communal settings and with having guests because it brings me back to that feeling of family. Like clockwork, one of the adults would wrangle together all of the kids after school and bring us home to eat snacks or take us to the recreation center around the corner. On any given day, dinner would turn into a feast reminiscent of Thanksgiving because folks from the neighborhood stopped by or my aunts felt like throwing down in the kitchen. We had a couple of refrigerators in the house that stayed full with everything from hot dogs to sausages, including steaks, biscuits, and pancakes, and an array of soul food, seafood, and pastas. The adults made sure the house never went empty. Now don't get me wrong; my first real taste of seafood did not come until adulthood. And steaks in restaurants were unheard of. Our steaks were for super-special occasions and cooked to the point you couldn't chew them.

The neighborhood knew and respected my family; it was a benefit I didn't fully grasp and appreciate until much later in life. I could go anywhere and people knew me or someone in my family, for better or worse. During fourth grade, I was threatened by a classmate for the first time. He said he was going to bring a gun to school the next week and force me to give him my shoes. And I believed him.

At that time, my half brothers and I were in a peculiar position. We were separated by households, but our dad always ensured we had the newest shoes, usually Air Jordans. And this was despite us living in an area where kids were getting maybe one or two pair of shoes the entire year. My dad wanted us to have the best of what he could offer. But to some select few who didn't know that backstory or see that we were also living in the same struggling economic class, our shoes were a reminder of privilege and of something they couldn't have.

Nothing came of the threat because my aunt Jackie seemed to know every person born in the city within three generations. One day, she saw me wearing an older pair of shoes and asked where my brand-new ones were. After much prodding, I reluctantly told her about the threat. Turns out, she knew exactly the child I was speaking of. His father immediately resolved the issue. I never did give over any shoes. I didn't ask any questions, and she promised I'd never have any trouble from him again. And, to this day, I never have.

Although this might seem like a success story, that experience taught me a much different lesson: never snitch. I was looked at differently after that by a number of students. I was definitely a figure to be avoided. They made comments under their breaths, and they did make certain days more challenging. The message was loud and clear.

Adversity at school wasn't new. I had transferred to Woodmore almost halfway through grade school. As a new student, I was the outsider who was not a part of any of the cliques that had been established in my absent months and years. That led to my own insecurities, and I always felt like I had a chip on my shoulder and had to assert myself as this runt who still felt like he was the shit. But I had to learn that you don't own the playground just because you're good at something, especially on new turf. I met some really great friends at Woodmore who showed me the ropes, including Jody, Quinntis, Adrian, Ricky, Jerry, Ivan, Dewayne, Jermichael, Larry, and the twins Christian and Christopher. They were good to me there and throughout middle and high school. I joked with them, hung out, played AAU basketball, went to school dances, and chatted about the fine girls with them.

These guys, each in his own way, managed to keep me from being a victim of unnecessary fights. One day, for example, I was determined to play a certain game at recess, and I didn't think it was right for this certain kid to always be the first to get to the games and claim them for himself or his buddies. I was the new kid, but I felt that I should be able to get whatever games I wanted. Little did I know that I was stirring the pot with the bully of the school. He had become a regular at the principal's office for detentions and suspensions. Jody pulled me to the side right before I was about to say something outlandish that was sure to earn me an immediate playground battle. He told me it wasn't worth it because the kid was a fighter with nothing to lose. He convinced me that I should avoid him and others like him. I'm thankful to Jody because, for years, I did just that and stayed out of harm's way.

I was a bright child by all the ways my teachers and family and friends measured it. At Woodmore, they began to pay real attention to what they deemed my advanced intellect. I was tested for the gifted program. I wish I had known as a child exactly what that meant, but I didn't and it hindered my abstract thought. I was given standardized tests and weird mapping and object placement tests where I had to put various blocks and shapes into very specific arrangements that would fit a pre-drawn diagram. I was also asked to interpret aloud various butterfly and parametric diagrams. All of this seemed very interesting and strange to me at first, but apparently I did well and was placed in the gifted program.

My new teacher was a gentle and patient white lady named Mrs. Wattenberger. She was very calm and intentional when she instructed us and gave us assignments and freedom to complete various tasks. The class met twice a week after lunch, and I would spend a couple of hours doing brain exercises or playing the renowned Oregon Trail computer game. I remember that, from time to time, we were given projects to complete in addition to our other classroom assignments.

I knew from a very young age that my interests were a little different from the rest of my family, peers, and friends. I'm grateful to my mom, dad, and grandmothers specifically for never hindering me from being the weird and outgoing child I was. They found a way for me to fit comfortably into the urban working class community. It was my safe haven.

Yet, they also did not hesitate to remind me about how things used to be. The sides of the city they couldn't visit in the past. The marches they interacted with and the law enforcement they encountered. I knew the inner-city life. I knew the wants and the needs, and the haves and have-nots; I knew what it meant for someone to fight for what they desired or what they needed as bare necessities. I knew people who smoked weed and crack, sold drugs, and boosted clothes. I knew more about the person in the neighborhood who was an expert at removing those ink and theft sensors than I did of the life of the hedge fund manager. But I could tell you how to make profit based on supply and demand. I knew the unspoken gestures and nods and handshakes that created acceptance in the tougher streets.

My guard was up in a different way around white people. I didn't have any daily interactions with white people, especially not peers. The imprint most blazed into my head was of the stories I had heard from aunts, uncles, and grandparents. Their tales were full of deceit, betrayal, brutality, and injustice. The American system we lived in was not built with us in mind. We were an afterthought, property. But I came from the cloth of fighters, who trained me to always fight for what I believed was right because each man is equal and no one deserves to take a back seat to anyone.

I think that complexity of life experience showed up in my gifted classroom. I would spend a lot of time by myself doing tasks and completing the games that we had on hand. Not in an isolated and lonely way. But more so in a way that helped me hone my problem-solving skills and the challenges that came with that. The gifted classes were the only times I could recall being challenged or intrigued by activities at school, outside of opportunities that involved playing sports or talking to friends.

Mrs. Wattenberger picked up on this and took a liking to me and my journey. Through a blessing of God, Mrs. Wattenberger received an opportunity at a middle school during my fifth-grade year. That new opportunity served dual purposes, as it turned out. My parents and Mrs. Wattenberger began to think of my next phase in middle school and the best educational opportunity. Mrs. Wattenberger was going to Hixson Middle School, a mixed but majority white school far from my district. It would take me thirty to forty-five minutes to get there. We had no way to make that happen, but we didn't let that deter our efforts.

CHAPTER 5:

HIXSON MIDDLE SCHOOL

"Several days Donté would come home from school and I'd be in the kitchen cooking or whatever. And he would be aggravating the kids. I would say, 'I need you to go get that telephone book for me and come sit right here by me while I'm cooking and read to me different people's names in the telephone book.' It was just to keep his attention. He has always wanted to be the smartest. He's always had that drive to do something and want to create something. Invent something. Tear stuff apart and put it back together. The type of person who's intrigued on how things work. I really enjoy him as a nephew. I always knew he had [the] drive to excel to be whatever he wanted to be." – Tresa Odom-Stripling, my aunt

We had no foreseeable way of making the commute to Hixson. By this time, my dad had been laid off from the engineering job he had landed after graduating from one of the top, black, technical high schools in the city. His job had served his kids well, but it also meant he never went to college to obtain his engineering degree. So when layoffs came around, he was the first to go. So went our usual standard of gifts and rewards for good grades in school.

Two years later, he enrolled in a bachelor's degree program for mechanical engineering. It was a great step forward, but it was also a strain on all parties, as time and money were cut very thin. Somehow, between my financial situation, tons of paperwork, tons of loopholes, and tons of vouching, Mrs. Wattenberger got me into Hixson. She had me classified as an exception in the gifted student program so my zoning was changed. She even figured out a way to have a bus pick me up to take me to and from school every day.

It was an interesting time. In addition to a new environment, I was balancing being a preteen and having my new stepfather, Arthur Tibbs, around more. My mom and Arthur crossed paths around 1990, not long after my sister and I were born. He had recently graduated from the HBCU Tuskegee University in 1989 with a degree in industrial technology and a minor in teaching. In college, he was a varsity swimmer and joined the Kappa Alpha Psi Fraternity, Inc. He gave me my first exposure to black college and fraternity experiences. I can remember being little and tagging along with him to fraternity probates and step shows at the University of Tennessee, Chattanooga. Those were my fondest memories of our time spent together.

We also connected on sports, one of our better connections. We would go to the gym or the fire station or the YMCA together to play pick-up basketball. I got to escape for a moment in the sport I loved while enjoying the camaraderie with him on the court. I did admire him being with my mom and his courage in taking on the weight of being a father figure to her children. It couldn't have been an easy task, but it was one he inched toward daily. His mother embraced me and my sister as her own grandchildren, as well. He was the eldest of two siblings, along with a close cousin who was raised with him because of a transfer of custody. I believe being the older sibling and father figure in his home while also being raised by a single mother led him to develop his own sense of authority. During my teen years, I was defiant of his strict approach and began to rebel against it all.

As the school year began at Hixson, I found myself among new classmates in a new environment with new peers and new challenges. This was the first time I had day-to-day interactions with white students of my age. It seemed like an okay situation. Over the course of my first year there, as a sixth grader, I had fun but I never made any lasting friendships. I met a couple of new friends through sports, most notably Tommie Paris. She was one of the best basketball players I have seen, and she continued to be throughout our middle school and high school years. But something just didn't pull me in at Hixson. I wasn't fully engaged in the schoolwork or the school's workings. Most of that year as a sixth grader is a blur. But there is one instance I wish I had the maturity and self-awareness and personal identity to deal with at the time.

As I mentioned earlier, I was categorized as a gifted student with special privileges that allowed me to also obtain daily transportation to and from school. Well, what I was unaware of at the time was this new categorization placed me in the same subset as our special needs students and students with learning disabilities. I was chauffeured to school on the infamous short bus. I felt so embarrassed by being dropped off at school with this group, especially as a new kid with no prior reference point for students or classmates to rely on. Mostly, my self-esteem was crushed, and my self-identity struggled to find its place. Not only were kids asking questions and making vile comments, but I also questioned where I belonged. Was I that different as a gifted student? Was I a social outcast for the way my brain worked?

I felt normal, but at Hixson I was being grouped with those deemed not normal. I could not understand why the way I learned was so different that I had to be separated into an entire subset of students who required individual attention and oversight. I questioned my place in all of this at a new school with new people. I cried and begged my mom not to make me ride that bus. I had a dear cousin who actually rode the very same bus with me. But I just couldn't conceive that I would be lumped in with students who were separated from other students. I disregarded the fact that my cousin was a very smart young man who needed more assistance, mainly due to his strabismus (the condition commonly referred to as cross-eyed where the individual cannot align both eyes simultaneously) and how he consumed information.

It wasn't until later in life that I could develop such an understanding of my own self-worth and security that I could have compassion and understanding for those with special needs and learning disabilities. I spent so much energy going out of my way to not be associated with a specific group of people. Looking back, I know I could have had a better experience had I just embraced the crowd and used that time to explain to others the issues plaguing children who are different. What I didn't realize was that my next journey in education would be an experience defined by differences as I entered a completely new world. A new level of difference, even beyond Hixson.

I remember mentioning the idea of attending a private school to my mom and dad. The memory sticks with me because during the same time I lost my Granny Ba-Ba, my maternal grandmother, on March 1, 1995. She was our matriarch and a central part of my childhood, so the change was felt deeply, especially as a preteen.

After I made my request, my parents took the initiative to contact Mrs. Wattenberger. There was a sense of trust, even hope, that my parents had developed from their experiences with her over time. I do not know exactly what her response was, but whatever it was, it resulted in my mom requesting an application packet and getting me signed up to take the entrance exam for The McCallie School for boys. My application marked the beginning of the nurturing relationship with the school's admissions officer, Susan Bailey. An application packet was mailed out to my mom, and she completed it almost immediately and mailed it back with the $100 application fee. Within a few weeks, I was scheduled to sit for the entrance exam the summer prior to my sixth grade year.

After I took the exam over the summer, Susan Bailey told my mom that she had more financial documents to complete in case I was accepted. The paperwork would ensure that I was eligible for a full scholarship. My mom frantically filled out the documents to meet the August deadline. After that, we heard nothing for months. The entire first semester of sixth grade passed while I attended Hixson and we had no communication from the admissions office at Mc-Callie. My mom and I both pushed the idea of a new school aside. Then on March 1, 1996, one year to the day of my grandmother's passing, my mother received a letter from McCallie in the mail. I had not only been accepted as an incoming student, but I would also be attending the school tuition-free. I am a firm believer that my acceptance and eventual experiences at McCallie were destined. It was a gift from God, maybe even a favor Granny Ba-Ba had called in. She had told me of my bright future at a private school before she passed. It was all meant to be.

CHAPTER 6:
THE MCCALLIE SCHOOL

"Donté has always had a smile on his face. Just being around Donté just makes you feel good. He's always been kind of cooler than me and just a guy I was always impressed with. He's consistent all the way through on integrity. We were raised in different family structures, but both of us had it driven into us from an early age to do the right thing. Donté has always seen the bigger picture and been going for that next step. It can be easy to be complacent and enjoy where you are. But Donté always keeps pushing and being outstanding, even when people he's hanging out with may not be as driven as he is."– Louis Anderson, my friend

In August of 1996, on my first day as a seventh grader at The Mc-Callie School for boys, I showed up in a perfectly starched navy-blue blazer, flawlessly creased khakis, a white shirt with a collar, a perfectly knotted tie, tan oxfords, and my obnoxiously oversized glasses. As I tried to navigate my way around the halls, I was greeted with confused stares and the occasional soft whispers. It wasn't until I found my locker and homeroom that things became clear, thanks to a fellow student who later became one of my best friends, Louis Anderson. In addition to being my first genuine white friend, Louis was a foundational and orienting pillar for my life at McCallie.

He is the product of a mother and a father who are passionate and intelligent and who gave birth to him and his sister in their early forties. He and his family were my first encounter with what has come to be labeled a cultural ally. His authenticity to himself and his belief in and passion for equal opportunity and treatment of individuals from all walks of life always impressed me.

We were not only study partners for eighty-five percent of our classes, but we were also basketball teammates for four of my six years at McCallie. We went on to serve as assistant basketball coaches together during our senior year. Louis's family, like mine, had some brief glory years with Tennessee Volunteers college sports teams. So, we spent many a day imagining a year where Tennessee would top the list of rankings and championships in all three major sporting events: football and men's and women's basketball. He's now married with a son, and I imagine Louis is raising him with those same values of equality, openness, work ethic, and SEC sports enthusiasm that brought us together. Louis not only allowed me to be myself without judgment but also was a peer who genuinely admired me and my work ethic against the backdrop of my life.

On that first day at McCallie, as I dropped my backpack down beside a sea of L.L. Bean bags, I knew then this was going to be quite a change and experience for me. I found my desk and locker, and beside me was this friendly and unassuming Louis. He must have seen the confusion and anxiety in my eyes as he introduced himself. He then said, "Why do you have your blazer on today? We only wear those on special occasions."

"Shit, I don't know," I replied. "My mom told me this was part of the uniform so I had to wear it."

At that moment, I knew I was about to learn a number of lessons I couldn't get at home. Louis kind of took me under his wing and continued to teach me and introduce me to experiences and phrases that were common among my new upper- and upper-middle- class peers. That seventh-grade year, I learned and experienced so much that was different from the microcosm I knew at my former schools and in my neighborhood.

It was in a conversation with Louis and a classmate whose father was a plastic surgeon in New York City that I got my first introduction to the vernacular of the rich. We were talking about something to do with prices, and my classmate kept saying the letter "k" after numbers. All I kept thinking to myself was, "What the hell is 'k'?"

So after he left, I asked Louis why he kept saying it. Louis responded, "He's a douche. It's just something rich people say that means a thousand."

From that moment, I made a point to pay even more attention and learn as much as I could, with Louis as my guide to keep me from any missteps. He did the same with me. As we bonded over school and athletics, Louis began to tell me just how much he admired and respected my work ethic and me. He would tell me I was one of the coolest, hardest-working, and smartest people he knew. Hearing words like that from him and, often, his family, too, reminded me that even beyond my race, clothes, vernacular, and more, there were people who saw me for me. Everything different about me was just a layer to invite them nearer for a closer look.

There is one occasion I've never let out of my mind. It was after spending a weekend at Louis's house. As the son of a pharmacist father and a career school teacher as a mother, Louis and Karen, his younger sister, lived a life very different from my own. They lived in Jasper, Tennessee, in Marion County. With a black population of just over two percent, on occasion there is still a sighting of the Confederate flag flying from flag poles and trucks alike. Much different from the black community in Chattanooga that I was accustomed to. I knew Louis was different, so the particulars of the town and its demographics did not unease me. My angst came at the realization of how different our upbringing had been. Something that dawned on me once we arrived at the Andersons' home.

The had a nice, modest home with a massive yard. The kind of yard where we could play tackle football on one side of the house, set up kickball field in the front yard, and career down a Slip 'N Slide on the other. I had never been to anyone's home that was that size; he and his sister had their own bedrooms and separate places for their toys so they never had to fight over playroom space. And both is parents were living in the same house and jointly engaged with their children's lives and their friends' lives as well. There was soda and snacks and pizza and popcorn and cookies and water guns and football and baseball and darts and pool tables. A weekend of fun I had not had the luxury of experiencing in one person's home prior to then. Before then, the only way I would have been able to experience all those activities was by attending the neighborhood recreation center. When the weekend was coming to an end, Louis's parents offered to drive me back home. A sense of angst came over me. Because we had left right from school, I never processed the fact that I had to get back home somehow. Immediately, I began to fear what could go wrong and how they would judge me. I wasn't ready for the raw dissection of my inner workings. I was still on guard because these were white people driving through a part of town they had never seen or heard of as far as I knew.

They would see rundown houses, trash spread along streets with no sidewalks, and guys hanging outside the corner store. That was outside of their norm. I was a product of a respected black family who had strong roots in black neighborhoods. I wasn't often ashamed of where I grew up or how I was raised. But that day was different. On one side, I had my pro-black community who were outwardly skeptical of anything and anyone who couldn't prove their blackness. And on the other side was my white best friend, who happened to be from a small town named Jasper thirty-eight miles from Chattanooga and had one stoplight.

Finally, to avoid any interrogation or awkward explanations on my behalf, I decided to have his parents drop me off at my grandmother's house. She lived only about two miles away from us, but the neighborhoods nearest her were much nicer and less threatening to outsiders. After being dropped off, I had a sense of shame. Not in the shame of where I came from, but in the shame that I didn't have the words or courage to express how I was feeling. Shame that I didn't recognize that the environment I grew up in with everything from the blatant cursing to the gritty determination were all part of my unique recipe. If you taste one ingredient of that recipe, it can leave a horrible taste in your mouth, but with the proper quantities of each and the right temperature and pressure, you can create a masterpiece the world can admire.

Looking back, I would have taken more time and made more opportunities for Louis to explore my neighborhood with me. I would've given him the chance to see why I got so excited when we played against the public schools, and let him get to know the same guys and friends I attended elementary school with and played basketball with throughout the city and in the summers. It was like a reunion for me every time our prestigious school would venture across the tunnel to play against the other schools.

I know he understood me and never judged me, but at the same time, I think I was still more cautious and leery of white people as a whole. I did not want to give them any leverage that would make them feel any type of pity for me or a sense of superiority for themselves. I just wished I could have been enriched even more as a young, black boy living in what seemed to be two different galaxies.

I do not believe there is any more valuable a lesson or gateway to success than exposure. Every step of my life has been paved or bypassed because of exposure. I have no doubt that I would have had much different and more monochromatic life experiences had I not gained the cultural exposure I received at McCallie during my teenage years. I learned what it meant to put education above everything else. We had our share of disciplinary issues, but nothing interfered with academics. It was as if every student knew it was a privilege to be in such an enriching culture and every student feared having to answer to their parents if things went too far.

I was surrounded by peers whose parents were doctors, lawyers, and businessmen at a top-five, premier boys secondary school with more than one hundred years of history in the South. The school prided itself on academics, athletics, and integrity. And, for six years, those principles were ingrained in my head. There was one lesson that was reinforced daily: All choices have consequences.

As I neared my sixteenth birthday, my peers and I "had gas on our breath," as they say back home. All we could think about was taking that driving test and getting our first car. But here was the difference between my classmates and me: they awaited a sparkling new vehicle or, at worst, a two-year-old, hand-me-down from their parents. I was hoping my family would just be willing to share the family car on the weekends so I could go to work and save to buy my own car, in addition to paying for gas and car insurance. I grew up around cars my whole life, but there was never a promise or guarantee I would have a car at sixteen years old. It reminded me what my dad had always taught me: if you want something, you make a way to get it. And that's what I did.

I am so Southern at heart. So at sixteen, true to the style of the '99 and 2000 as rapper Juvenile says it, all I wanted was a candy-painted Oldsmobile Cutlass Supreme with 20-inch wheels. But, being the flashy kid of an engineer, I also wanted it to be high-tech. It had to have the best sound system because I like my rap Southern: loud and full of bass. I set out to get all of that. I started by getting my license by way of my grandmother because my mom was against the idea of me driving with little experience. But what she didn't know was that I had been driving with my father since I was twelve years old. Nonetheless, that summer I got my license and started to work, and I continued during the weekends after school started. After battling week in and week out with my mother, who felt disappointed and slighted that I went to get my license without her permission and who wasn't the one to get to enjoy the pleasure of my success with me, I was forced to wait. It was kind of a lesson in obedience.

In the meantime, I managed to save enough money to fund the gas, insurance, and extras I wanted in my car. I was allowed to drive my mom's ten-year-old truck. When I started driving, my car insurance was under my mother's policy. This was a major point of contention because of the added cost of the insurance and the added financial burden it would place on the family. As soon as I was able to contribute to that monthly bill, I offered up the funds to help cover my portion.

I was still making it better than most of the guys in my neighborhood because at least my mom could afford to give me her old truck. I also gained a level of responsibility and humbleness by driving the truck and having to finance everything that came with owning a car, from oil changes to new speakers, tires, and a CD player. It was my first real responsibility. That experience of independence guided me through the next decade of my life.

I went to school, played basketball, and worked. My routine was going from Wendy's to Baskin-Robbins to Just for Feet to Blockbuster. I would separate my week by dividing my time between each of the various jobs as long as I could sustain it. I would usually work about four hours at a time at each facility, which was what the child labor laws then allowed. I was able to do about five to ten hours per week at each job. That would add up to twenty to thirty hours of work each week.

At my high school, I was the exception. In my neighborhood, it was a rite of passage and an expectation. My classmates went home and had family dinner, getting caught up on the issues of the day with their parents. I worked until 9:00 p.m. and came home to finish up schoolwork. I knew my path was different, but it didn't mean I couldn't absorb lessons and bullet points from those around me.

I must confess I have never had an issue with parents who to gift their teenager a nice vehicle. If I'm afforded the opportunity, I will probably do the same. But I do know the work I had to endure made me value the privilege much more, and it also spilled over into other areas of my life.

A work ethic produces results. I didn't get that Cutlass I wanted or a newly painted car, but I did manage to buy various upgrades for my mom's Ford Explorer, including twelve-inch subwoofers and a multidisc CD player.

While at McCallie, which has been ranked among the top five all-boys schools in the US, I developed a new awareness of my identity. I was allowed to explore the differences of my maturity as a black male within the confines of this all-white microcosm of reality. It was here that I pushed the rules with earrings and facial hair, both of which were not within the dress code. The earrings were something I had always wanted as a child, being that it was a trend during the eighties and nineties.

But the facial hair was something completely different. I come from a family of heavily bearded men, and I didn't think much of that until I got to be about fourteen. As hair began to faintly show up on my face, I would try from time to time to shave it off completely as our dress code required. But every time I did, my face took on this weird appearance of an eight-year-old. My closest friends at school often made fun of me after those shaving experiments. But I think beyond that, my professors and coaches saw the huge difference as well. I don't think it helped that I was 110 pounds with lips that appeared out of proportion when left free of the shade of a light mustache. So I was given little grief for not shaving, as long as I kept my facial hair very light and not lumberjack-like.

McCallie also allowed me to push the envelope by expressing myself. During my sophomore and junior years, I got bold enough to push the limits and grow out my hair into this massive Afro that would routinely be transformed into cornrows of various designs. As most young boys and basketball players of that time, I made Allen Iverson one of my favorites following Michael Jordan's departure from the NBA. He was the small-in-stature rebel defeating all odds and climbing over every obstacle put his way. I saw myself in him, from the inner-city athletic black kid attending prep school to the world of possibilities that lay ahead of him, if only he could stay out of trouble and free of the turmoil that members of his entourage could bring forth down the line. I loved the braids and tats, and the way women swooned over him and his uncompromising attitude. No one was going to put him in a box and make him be something he was not. I took that belief to heart.

It helped that I had been raised to be myself and to be confident with who I was, without apology. McCallie was the perfect petri dish for that growth and expression. At times, it did get me in trouble, though. Once, I got released from the strength-training program because I refused to commit to the daily process. I was consumed with feeling unappreciated as a basketball player. I felt that my teammates had a system I was never going to be allowed to break through because they had all grown up together in their elementary school leagues and summer leagues, whereas I, in turn, was playing with the inner-city leagues. My father didn't have access to coaches the same way these other players' parents did. And after five years with little improvement in the roster beyond sixth man, I thought I wasn't being given my fair share.

Things got even rockier after I decided to work a summer job instead of going to camp with the rest of the basketball team. I believe my coach felt that this was a selfish decision on my part and not the actual financial decision it was because of my family's income level. I had to work to support myself, and the added $700 of team camp was not ever going to be a priority over my stability as a person during that time. I rebelled, or, as I saw it, I survived and chose a different path. This sacrifice and the result were not without their benefits.

It was during my senior year that Louis, who had previously stopped playing basketball after being cut from the team, and I were offered assistant coaching positions at McCallie for the seventh-grade basketball team. It was one of the most fun, exciting, and fulfilling jobs I have ever had. I was used to caring for kids of that age bracket, as I had been a summer camp worker for a number of years prior. But I realized I had a passion for coaching and pushing kids to become the best they can be while giving them hands-on tips on techniques and aspects of the game. It was great to see that team grow and develop throughout the season as we went undefeated. Later, a couple of the players went on to play Division I sports, and one was even drafted to the NFL as a quarterback.

Choosing to tackle these inner dilemmas of sacrifice and survival in my own way has always left me more satisfied than if I had gone about it in a different manner. I can always deal with the consequences when I know the choice I made was my own. I know my experiences would have been much more stimulating had I not endured these life lessons as a teenager. But I do believe it made me understand the roles of money, bills, and fiscal responsibility as I learned to budget and stretch what little money I was making. These lessons played a part in my decision about where to go for college as I went through my senior year.

As I was maturing and absorbing information around me, both from my family and the family members of my classmates, I began to appreciate the benefits of creating multiple streams of income. I leveraged this when it came to the cost of my education. As I grew older and nearer to my senior year, it became apparent that no one was going to be footing the bill for my college education.

My family didn't have the typical college fund set up for me. My parents were not going to be writing a check to any institution on my behalf to cover the cost of my education. We were paying for light bills and dial-up internet and food; there was no money for family dinners out or family vacations, let alone a separate savings account for any of the children's college educations. So while most of my classmates were thinking about which school they were going to attend and the fun they were going to have while there, I was already thinking of how I was going to pay for college once I finished. There was no safety net going into college, and there certainly wasn't going to be one coming out of it either.

Everything, my relationship with my mother, my relationship with my stepfather, my endless work schedule, had actually been a spiral until that point. During my senior year, my childhood bedroom and furniture had been transformed. What previously had been a private teenage cave covered wall to wall with one hundred posters of Michael Jordan, including the life-size, standing cardboard cutout, was transformed. Out with my boyhood memories—including Michael Jordan—and in with the bedroom suite of my mom and stepfather.

I did, however, envision my parents sharing in the financial responsibility by at least partnering with me and co-signing for whatever loans I might need to make my dreams come true. During my senior year, I found out I was honored as a National Achievement finalist because of my scores on the Preliminary Scholastic Aptitude Test (P/SAT), an exam that serves as a practice test for the Scholastic Aptitude Test (SAT), which is a tool used to access students' preparedness for college admissions. I was ranked among the highest scorers among black students throughout the nation. With this new title and my GPA came a plethora of scholarship offers and fee waivers for college applications. We were ecstatic about the fee waivers, being that those fees served as another barrier for lower-income families for admittance into an institution. If a person can't afford to cast the net, they may be forced to accept any offer or to accept a rejection because of the mere inability to afford the application fee. I turned in numerous applications and received scholarship offers from all but one, Emory University.

At McCallie, our guidance counselor would go over our grades and standardized test scores and rank our various university and college options. Although I ranked high in the world of achievement by national standards, I felt completely average and non-extraordinary around my peers. As a student at a prestigious middle school and high school, I always thought I was an average student, ignoring the fact that I was surrounded by some of the brightest boys in the country.

You measure yourself by your competition, and, though my grades far exceeded average, I felt nothing grand about my accomplishments. Not realizing that my average could very well be spectacular in any normal setting, I didn't apply to any Ivy League schools. It was a decision I later regretted. After all the acceptance letters were received, my choice came down to two schools: the prestigious, all-male historically black college and university (HBCU) Morehouse College or Oxford College of Emory University. On one side of the coin was a full presidential scholarship to Morehouse College, on the other, a seventy-five percent scholarship and financial package to Emory. Here is where my road in life diverged from the course of the other students at McCallie and my other male peers who attended Morehouse.

CHAPTER 7:
OXFORD COLLEGE OF EMORY UNIVERSITY

"One thing I've always noticed about Donté is, he's going to do his own thing, regardless of whether or not other people are doing it. He always was a trendsetter, from his style to academic things. I've started to see he is more willing to ask for help and not take on everything and burn himself out. Donté is genuinely a good person. He's very dependable, whether it's going on trips, needing advice, or just needing help. You can always call on him." – Dr. Thomas "TJ" Jefferson IV, my friend

In the spring of 2002, my senior year of high school, I accepted the full scholarship to Morehouse College. In April, I went down for an incoming-student day to visit the campus before classes began that fall. I had come to feel like I was supposed to be a Morehouse Man over the course of my senior year. But something inside of me wasn't sitting quite so well with the decision after my visit. Maybe it was the ideology of turning boys into men, which I felt I had fully achieved having been through similar development while at my secondary school. Or maybe it was the staunch pro-black rhetoric. Or the enormous supervision and restrictions placed upon the incoming students. Whatever it was, I never quite came to grips with that choice. By midsummer, I had changed my mind and withdrew my acceptance of the scholarship.

In turn, I chose a university a few miles away from Morehouse College, just outside of Atlanta. I felt more comfortable with it as a whole for my continued growth and experiences: Oxford College of Emory University.

Being free to make decisions on my own was ultimately a major factor in my decision to not attend Morehouse. By the time I made my college decision, I was already more independent than most of my peers and some adults. I knew that once I left my home in Chattanooga I would not be back as an inhabitant. The day I left for college was the last day I would rely on my family. My departure defined my transition from being a liability to a provider, for myself and my family.

The summer right before college, I was given a luggage collection. For me that meant, once I was gone, I was *gone*. It was time to be a man and no longer my parents' responsibility. There was a room and a bed in Chattanooga for me, but they were not *mine*. Adding all of this to my subconscious and maybe conscious feeling that I would never live to be thirty as a black man in America made the weight of my new adulthood heavy.

I didn't want anyone dictating what I could or couldn't do because no one knew what I was up against except me. I didn't need the hand-holding because no one was going to feed me or make me successful except me, by my own merit and ambition. I didn't need the preplanned road map or institutionalized blinders put in place to ensure that young adults didn't fly off track or lose their way. I already had experience in making my own decisions in the world to find a way to get what I wanted.

August 2002 arrived, and it was time for freshman orientation week. That's where my dependence ended and my independence took root. My life was forever changed. There was one defining moment and conversation I believe solidified how I now carry myself. During orientation, I closed the door on seeking permission for anything and asking for assistance in any way to survive. As many kids, parents, and guardians can attest, that first week of college is a whirlwind of emotions. Kids are gearing up to experience their first piece of freedom and responsibility while parents are being forced to cut ties and allow their babies to spread their wings and explore the world.

In Oxford, Georgia, I was geeked, enjoying the introductions while also beginning to learn the importance of diplomacy and compromise with roommates. During the first day of orientation, also move-in day, there was a financial aid seminar for incoming freshman and parents to get answers on grants, loans, work study, etc. It also allowed students and parents the opportunity to sit in on Q&A sessions and inquire about future or available scholarships for students in their prospective fields. My mom and stepfather attended these financial seminars with me. After reviewing my financial aid summary, we saw that after my scholarship was applied, there was still going to be a shortage of about $10,000 a year. Prior to that, we hadn't really discussed financing college or what the plan was going to be. But shortly after the session, it became very clear.

As we were exiting the rotunda, my stepfather asked, "How are you planning to pay for school?"

It was a question I was definitely ill-prepared for, and, quite frankly, I had no answer or solution. If you recall, this relationship between my stepfather and I was not the most stable beyond the superficial sports and occasional outings. And I had assumed that my immediate family would be supportive of my decisions, both symbolically and financially. Was this not a team effort on behalf of everyone that I might have successful matriculation into college like the rest of my peers? Were they not happy I chose a prestigious school that would foster my growth and success?

In a state of bewilderment and confusion, I simply replied, "Huh?"

He replied, "Are you taking out loans or something? Because I'm not signing my name to nothing. You need to talk to the financial aid office and figure out your options."

"What does that mean for me?" I asked.

"You got to figure it out. You wanted to be here, so find out how to be here. We're not signing up for any loans, and we're not cosigning any loans," he asserted.

I looked to my mom for support or backup, but she stared back at me blankly. No response. No emotion. No reaction. A poker face. It was a surprise to me. A surprise I received after having moved everything out of my former home in Chattanooga and into my dorm. There was nowhere for me to turn. My dad was just getting settled into his new job after years of low-wage jobs to stay afloat while taking classes to finish his engineering degree, and he had accrued his own student loans. There was no money in that corner, either. It was all or nothing for me, right then and there. And it was then that I shut off emotions and went into my soon ever-present survival mode.

I knew we were not well off, but I had still expected my mom and stepdad to share the responsibility for my education, finances, and survival as a new college student. I, naively or wishfully, had thought that we would share the burden, if not directly by writing a check, at least indirectly by co-signing on a loan with me if necessary.

I now realized just how little I knew about the financial workings of not only the collegiate education system but also of the financial burdens and ramifications of the banking system as it pertained to borrowers and cosigners. I knew nothing, and because of that I was unprepared and saw myself at a disadvantage. I swallowed what pride I had and everything went numb. From there, it was all tunnel vision as I reached out to financial counselors and visited the bursar's office on a quest to figure out what recourse an admitted student had for getting the funds needed to attend college.

I didn't have time to sulk or negotiate; all I had were my instincts and myself. After making the first completely solo adult decision, everything changed in my relationship with my family and my dependency on them. After that day and that moment, I was entirely void of desire to ask for permission or for financial help from family near and far. If I was going to do anything or need anything, I was going to make a way to get it myself.

During my freshman year, my mom and stepfather announced they had filed for divorce. It was a total surprise to me, but maybe it was because I was fully engaged in life at home to pick up on any of the signs of hardship within the marriage. My time away for college only increased that distance of involvement within the family, so to me, everything seemed stable. Though their marriage ended, he remained cordial with me and my family. I guess it's hard not to be when you've been a staple in someone's life for more than a decade.

As a freshman, I pursued work-study jobs. I was willing to do almost anything to stay afloat and to remain independent, all while flourishing and enjoying my freedom as a college student. I befriended cafeteria workers, and it helped that I was one of the few black students who was actually social and outgoing. They always knew where and how to find me, and from time to time they would share extra desserts, snacks, or meals with me or hold a plate for me after hours if they knew I was going to be late for dinner because of my work or school schedule.

My first four semesters, I took eighteen credit hours each semester, became a member of the Freshman Council, served as vice president of the Student Government Association (SGA), joined the Black Student Alliance, and made the Dean's List. I also worked as an assistant for the dean of the university, became a teacher's assistant for an anatomy and physiology class, and worked as a breakfast cook at night at our on-campus café. I did whatever it took to accomplish my goals of being independent while also being a leader among my peers.

That challenge of financial aid sparked a fire in me that not only shut off emotions and expectations from the rest of the world but also fueled me to take every opportunity possible in order to advance. I couldn't not eat, so I worked. I couldn't call home for an allowance, so I worked. I couldn't leave campus for trips and vacations, so I worked. I couldn't afford a tutor, so I worked. I had very little sleep in those days, often staying up late to study while friends and classmates were fast asleep or enjoying college thrills. I wasn't afforded the luxury of procrastination because every moment had to be accounted for. I allowed myself no leisure time until all my obligations had been satisfied. Yes, I was very social, but, first and foremost, I had to be a scholar and a financially responsible young adult. These earlier semesters and experiences molded me into what I needed to be to stay grounded and motivated.

Since I'd been at McCallie, I had been set on the medical school path. But the problem I encountered was a lack of guidance from my family and my network. I had one friend whose parents were doctors, but beyond that I had no one to look up to or any road map to follow as to what was needed or expected of me to enter the world of medicine. What I knew was, there was no room for error, and I couldn't leave my fate in the hands of a possibility. I knew I was a good student, but I never internalized a true measure of success. I didn't have a built-in sense of self-esteem that told me I was guaranteed an acceptance into medical school. And beyond that, I couldn't fathom how I was going to survive financially from undergrad to med school through residency and beyond. Yet I could not imagine my life if I didn't get into med school.

In the full spirit of survival and preparedness, I had to come up with a plan to support myself in the event I didn't get into med school. That's when I began to take nursing under strong consideration. With a degree in the nursing field, I knew I could create a sustainable foundation. I knew the core curriculum and prerequisites would align with those for med school while at the same time putting me in a position to secure a career if things didn't go as planned.

Nursing was the clear option that would allow me the time and opportunity to have the largest impact, freedom, and success in my life. And in hindsight, it was a much better decision for me to attend Emory than Morehouse, given they did not offer pre-nursing or nursing as a major. During my freshman year, I officially declared my major as nursing. The plan was to get my bachelor's, take the Medical College Admission Test *(MCAT*), and attend medical school following graduation.

God laughed at these plans.

* * * *

To add some background, Oxford College of Emory University in Oxford was the original birthplace of what's now Emory University in Atlanta. Oxford was a blur of early morning classes, whiskey, streaking hallways of the dorms in late-night adrenaline rushes, and senseless disregard for authority. It was the ultimate point of freedom in my life. It allowed me to fully embrace the outgoing and act-first-regret-later mantra that has defined my life since childhood.

During my freshman and sophomore years, I got my first passport. I didn't get it for myself but for a future college sweetheart, Fern D'Leah Carty, or Leah as I knew her. She was a West Indian Caribbean-born young lady from St. Croix in the US Virgin Islands. We met for the first time on the final day of freshman orientation and were inseparable from that point on. In one way or another, we became each other's stability, first as friends and then as more.

Leah had a humble upbringing, raised in part by one aunt in St. Croix whom she called Mom, and through her adolescence by her aunt in south Atlanta. She exposed me to West Indian culture; I exposed her to Southern charm and hospitality. As a very young child, she had lost both her mother and father in traumatizing freak accidents. Her aunts demanded she have polite manners and injected a sense of debutante-like elegance in how she carried herself. These characteristics were something I learned from, and she also helped broaden my experiences and palate in music, travel, culture, and more.

Leah was the first person I met who was humble even after having enjoyed more privileged experiences behind closed doors, fortunate to have been invited to various galas and private dinners and fundraisers via her family's close ties to the local government and municipality. She also attended private schools where her peers were the sons and daughters of government officials, members of city councils, congressmen/women, and philanthropists. She was the first person who impressed upon me the notion that you can say more quietly than by screaming or with gaudy materials.

Having been born in St. Croix and having traveled back and forth to the US, she had always known life with a passport. So she found it unbelievable that I didn't own one and I hadn't been to the Caribbean. I told her that no one I knew growing up had a passport or had placed any importance on having one. At that time, I had only been on a plane twice, and that was on a roundtrip flight from Chattanooga to Akron, Ohio.

Leah made it her mission to offer me travel experiences at least two times a year. After she sat me down and forced me to fill out the passport application, we made a number of trips to the Caribbean, ranging from the US Virgin Islands and the British Virgin Islands to the Grand Bahamas. These experiences allowed me to not only round out my knowledge, but they also motivated me to progress up the ladder of success so that I could continue to enjoy this lifestyle.

Also while at Emory, Leah, at the age of twenty, bought her own condo in Atlanta. It was my first up-close experience of the ups and downs of a home search and purchase. Little did I know this would open my eyes to the wide world of opportunity in real estate. I can thank her for my first foray into wealth development and asset allocation and diversification.

After college, Leah went on to law school at Arkansas University. We ended our relationship then, but we have remained cordial over the years. She has served as general counsel at Walmart, and she most recently relocated to Houston with her own family.

Leah fed my hunger for West Indian culture and nurtured my love for reggae and Caribbean food. I have since never missed a year without attending at least one Carnival. I am a true believer that a passport is the best gift any preteen or adolescent can receive. Before I met Leah, the world for me was no larger than a state or two beyond Tennessee. I couldn't process a world over an ocean or even how to get there.

I am always in awe everywhere I go. It's all an escape. My imagination runs free, and I feel this amazing liberation when I get outside of America. I love my country, I love my state, and I love the city I grew up in, but I am not ignorant of or unscathed by the horrors of our history. Nor do I cover my eyes to the realities and pains and hardships that still haunt black people as well as the poor, women, members of the LGBTQ community, non-Christians, and any other minority who doesn't fit the mold of our Founding Fathers: white, Christian, and male.

At Oxford, I picked up the entrepreneurial reins from my father. During my freshman and sophomore years, I founded my first company, Fly Society Enterprises LLC, and marketed weekly, themed parties for the students. The parties featured DJs from throughout the region and allowed students an outlet off-campus where we could party in a club setting. Initially, the parties were targeted to the Oxford and Emory students. But, as time went on, my team collaborated with other notable promoters in the Atlanta area, as well as in Tallahassee and Birmingham. Together, we hosted parties, small concerts, and festivals that featured rappers, singers, musicians, and athletes. I also had the pleasure to host a few corporate events for both Emory University as well as Emory Healthcare. During my junior and senior years, we hosted Atlanta's First Fridays and New Year's Eve parties at the Fox Theatre. It was a great experience to be part of the transition of Atlanta's club and bar scene from 2002 to 2006, when the city was seeing the conversion of Buckhead from a party hub to luxury shops and condos.

I am grateful for college experiences like my first skydive, which took place in east Alabama at 14,000 feet. During my sophomore year, I also decided to do something unimaginable, at least not imaginable to some of my peers and more conservative adults. I agreed to be a weekly nude model for an advanced art class. My time in undergrad was right before the burgeoning of social media and listservs and mass online marketing. At Emory, we used the online community of Blackboard for course materials and assignments. Through Blackboard's integrated system, students could also create their own groups and databases for campus communications or private group forums and chats. One of these campus-wide groups was titled Classifieds, and, like the local newspaper, anyone could post potential job openings or employment opportunities.

One day, I was considering ways to fill my free time (the three to four hours I had on Friday afternoons waiting on classmates to get done with their courses) in the upcoming semester. I decided to see what the classifieds had available, and, when I saw the icon for art it caught my attention. Initially, I thought working for the art department would be a mindless job, maybe filing or organizing the art studios or possibly sweeping and mopping the floors. To my surprise, when I opened the ad, I found a weekly job opening for a nude model in the advanced drawing class. My first reaction was, "This seems interesting."

I'm naturally an opportunistic person who loves adventure, so it just seemed like one of those chances that doesn't present itself in routine life. I didn't know anyone who had posed nude for an art class. Yet the idea of being nude was easy. Part vanity, part curiosity, part adventure, and part exploration led me to immediately email the professor and say I was interested.

I think she might have been more nervous than I was. I don't think she expected the ease with which I approached the role. She reassured me about the privacy of the room, professionalism of the students involved, and comfortable temperature of the studio. Literally, step-by-step, she explained the structure of the class to me. The students would spend the week learning a new drawing or painting technique in various mediums. On Fridays, I would be their model and allow them to explore those new techniques. The class was three hours long, which meant I posed motionless, occasionally in an action pose with various props.

It was meditative for me. It was one of the few times in my life I've been still, totally exposed both literally and metaphorically. I would get undressed in the adjoining bathroom and walk into the classroom wrapped in a towel-skirt and await my instructions from the professor regarding my role for the day. Then I would drop my towel and climb up on to this makeshift stage in the center of the classroom and my mind would just go clear. I would close my eyes, take a deep breath, and try to pick one item in the distance to affix my gaze on for the duration of the class. Time seemed to stop for me during those hours. Most of my peers didn't know about the modeling for at least a semester or two, even though one of my friends unexpectedly walked in on the class and saw me onstage in a full frontal; she completely covered her eyes and lowered her head as she made her way to the professor. As an advanced artist herself, she later became a student in the same class. To this day, I wish I had kept some of the phenomenal pieces she created during the semester she spent in that class.

Modeling nude remains one of the most exhilarating experiences I've had the pleasure to enjoy. Not only did I ace anatomy and physiology and become a teacher's assistant (TA) for the course, where I helped tutor and reinforce lessons taught by the professor as well as lead the students on laboratory days, but I was also the resident model and earned a nominal fee. The decision to model wasn't about the money. It was about doing something taboo. I knew it would force people to look at nude modeling differently. To this day, this is my go-to icebreaker in group settings or leadership meetings because it's the last thing people expect to hear. But ,like many things in my life, I'm not an open-and-shut book. I like challenging people to dive deeper, beyond appearances, titles, and complexions to see who someone is as a person.

My work-study job while at Oxford also proved to be impactful. I was the student assistant to the dean of Oxford College. I would file papers or run errands across campus as well as collate documents and prep materials for meetings and events. In the position, I met and worked alongside three of the most fabulous secretaries ever. It was like every day I was sitting on the set of *The Golden Girls*. Each secretary had been employed at the college for thirty-plus years, so there was nothing and no one they didn't know. They were an invaluable asset to my experiences both on and off campus, from gossip and Southern nurturing to direct access to the dean to their genuine curiosity about my life.

After causing mayhem on the six hundred-student campus of Oxford, I applied and got accepted into the nursing program at Emory University as a junior.

CHAPTER 8:
NURSING PROGRAM
AT EMORY UNIVERSITY

"Donté was one of my students and worked in the Emory skills lab where I taught some of the fundamental clinical skills. As his academic advisor, I observed his career in nursing unfold. He demonstrated a lot of leadership—always involved and taking initiative. He had really good interpersonal skills and was always the connector. Donte's a networker, an optimistic person with an entrepreneurial spirit. He was much more dimensional than those nursing students who were just there to get through a course. I see him now, and I see his ability to advocate, engage, motivate, and inspire other people. Research is showing it's important that the role models, teachers, and people who take care of you, such as nurses, look like you and understand you. And here we have Donté, an inspiring leader who is a black man in nursing. He is well positioned to make significant contributions."– Dr. Corrine Abraham

My plan, which was still focused on eventually going to med school, was not much different than that of my peers in the program.

But, at first, I hated the program because of its new way of learning. In 2004, I came into nursing as a Type A student, overachieving and highly motivated. I had no fear of failing or being remotely unsuccessful in this realm.

Boy, did I underestimate things. The science of nursing felt pretty intuitive, but, as any student of any nursing program can tell you, the subjective testing is different. It was unlike anything I'd experienced from secondary school and post-secondary school on up through those first two years of college. Tests were given over hundreds of pages of information, but all the test questions were based on best-answer dynamics. What this meant for the unsuspecting student was that not only were there multiple proper answers for each and every question, but there was one best answer chosen by the professor. This way of testing was a curveball for most of the students in my class, and, upon talking to students in other classes, had been this way for decades of nursing programs across the country and in different institutions.

Now, the model would have been manageable had professors explained the design prior to the beginning of classes and tests. But that was not the case. I spent two semesters cringing at every test debriefing, knowing the answers I had chosen were correct but were subject to the professor's scrutiny and decision-making. There was much debate about whether any credit should be given or if partial credit should be given.

Every post-test day was the same. I'd go to class, sit in my chair, and dread the reading of every question and answer, only to accept a final grade in the seventies in the end. Then I would leave with no idea how to improve. Professors were not helpful, past students were not helpful, and classmates couldn't explain the rights and wrongs of the testing.

Then, things changed during my third semester, thanks to one adjunct professor, Jill Hamilton. She was a blunt, straightforward, no-games black woman. And in her class, she gave us the secret to nursing school. But you had to be paying attention to catch it.

She said, "It's all about prioritizing! Everything we do is about prioritizing. What goes first? What's most important? And it begins with the ABCs."

This statement set a light bulb off in my head and made everything so clear. I was still frustrated, though. Good, strong, intelligent, and well-intentioned students were being weeded out semester after semester, not because they couldn't get the material but because they couldn't think critically about priorities. I'd learned material day after day and answered question after question correctly on tests, only to be told there was a more correct answer. It destroyed my psyche.

I still have an enormous disdain for nursing programs for young adults as well as introductory nursing jobs that follow similar teaching and training practices. Both go to the common phrase that "nurses eat their young." Many of my peers from schools across the country and I experienced a lack of mentoring, nurturing, and guidance.

Many experienced nurses don't feel the way I do. Some of those feelings come from a place of "Well, I had to go through it, and they should, too!" Or "It's the only way they're going to get better and stronger and learn what actions to take and not take."

Much research has been done in the realm of faculty civility as it relates to interactions with students in nursing programs. Dr. Cynthia M. Clark, PhD, RN, ANEF, FAAN, has spent much of her career researching and advocating for improved cultures within nursing and has even been a lead on the team that created a tool called the Workplace Civility Index to assess the work environment. Dr. Clark addressed the subject head-on in her 2008 publication, "The Dance of Incivility in Nursing Education as Described by Nursing Faculty and Students." In the article, both faculty and students describe their personal experiences with bullying and incivility within the education system and how it is used to "weed out" the less strong students. In another article, "Student Voices on Faculty Incivility in Nursing Education: A Conceptual Model," Dr. Clark uses a phenomenological method to perform a qualitative study in which three common themes emerged: feeling traumatized, feeling powerless and helpless, and feeling angry and upset.

One mistake could mean life or death for any number of people, and we're asking our new graduates to flourish in this situation. Who wouldn't be scared of an irreversible mistake? Who wouldn't need encouragement and further teaching in real-life scenarios? Where are our mentor programs? Why doesn't the nursing profession lift up the newcomers as future leaders of tomorrow? The *2008 National Sample Survey of Registered Nurses* not only found that the majority of employed nurses are between the ages of forty-five and fifty-nine, but that average age of a registered nurse in the United States is fifty years old. If we continue to push the younger students and nurses away by throwing them in the deep end to sink or swim, who's going to be here to care for us in our later years in life?

In my third semester in the nursing program, my professional trajectory diverted away from medical school as I became a clinical student on the mother-baby ward of the labor and delivery floor at Crawford Long Hospital. Nursing students were required to take six- to eight-week rotations through various hospital units and specialty areas as a way to gain hands-on experience in nursing as well as to implement the knowledge we learned in classes. Labor and delivery and mother-baby are among those specialty areas, which include pediatrics, renal, medical-surgical, cardiac, and oncology. Students are expected to gain a comprehensive experience of all areas of nursing and of all the various opportunities that lie ahead.

As a twenty-year-old male, I had a difficult time getting the proper experience while doing this rotation. When it came to labor and delivery and the expectant mother, patients', their significant others', or their parents' privacy and preconceived notions of my inadequacy did not allow me to take advantage of this learning opportunity. I distinctly remember a mother, in her protective state, dismissing my clinical background and schooling as a nurse and refusing to allow me to examine her daughter, who was completely cooperative with me and had given consent to preceptors and instructors for me to be part of the clinical activities during the shift.

This became the theme of my time on the unit. I spent more time in nursing lounges or at empty nursing stations reading textbooks than gaining actual hands-on experience. Every time I was denied an experience, I couldn't help but think I was being seen as a hormone-driven college boy or as some clinician looking to sexually assault or disrespect my patient. This made me even more uncomfortable as I tried to describe to new mothers the proper techniques and tips for breastfeeding and how to get an uncooperative newborn to latch on. No matter how correct my explanation was, I was often dismissed as not being qualified to discuss the matter. It was not lost on me that many of these patients had male ob-gyns and participated in exams that included residents who were learning. I came to realize that this was one of the first times I outright experienced a societal double standard, given the pedestal on which we place professional titles and the white coat.

In the midst of these experiences, someone took notice of me and gave an invitation that changed the course of my career. One day, while I was sitting at the front desk reading clinical texts, a woman in scrubs and a bonnet approached me and asked what I was doing. I assumed she knew I was an Emory student, given our standout navy scrubs, but I answered her anyway and told her I was hanging out on my labor and delivery rotation, waiting to assist people wherever they might need me.

She said, "But, you're reading a book. That can't be too exciting. How about you come spend the rest of the day with me?"

Well, it's not like I have anything else to do.

I said sure, and she immediately went to find my preceptor to get permission for me to leave the unit. She got me dressed in proper surgical attire, complete with scrub hat and mask, and she explained her nursing role. It was then that she, Debra Warth, or Debbie as many people called her, encouraged me to consider Certified Registered Nurse Anesthetists (CRNA) school. I had never heard of this nursing specialty. And this conversation was all happening in the midst of us preparing to take a patient to the operating room for a Cesarean section.

While she was gathering the drugs and materials needed for a spinal block, she was proclaiming all the benefits and challenges and accomplishments that come with pursuing a master's degree in nurse anesthesia. Debbie explained the privilege I would have in relieving patients' pain and the honor I would get from patients who surrendered power and control as they entrusted their lives to me. She was so excited about her career choice and was very honest about the stressors that come with the job, such as potential death and hospital politics. She explained I would get exposure to patients at all levels and develop the skill set to work both as a team member and an autonomous clinician. We discussed the various hands-on skills and techniques I would get to employ during my studies and career, depending on where I practiced after graduation. The road was not going to be easy, she said, but I had an opportunity to do something not many accomplished.

Debbie was very candid and told me, "You're a young, black man in nursing at a well-known program. Your image means a lot to who you are, and schools will be elated to have you in their program. Use that to your advantage, and be sure to pull others up with you."

I had not expected such clear direction from a white woman about how I had a chance to make a much larger difference in my profession by taking advantage of the position I was in as a black male. The words from our first day together were enough to push me to research the profession and take the initial steps toward becoming a nurse anesthetist. From that day forward, I shadowed Debbie two times a week in the labor and delivery suite for C-sections.

I did the research that led me down the path of job satisfaction, and I looked at the career options and requirements necessary to get admitted into a top-rated master's program. I saw great compensation options and job satisfaction ratings consistently above ninety percent year after year, and I was sold.

As I did my research, I would ask staff nurses what they thought of the nurse anesthesia field. The responses I received were polar opposites of one another. There was never a lukewarm opinion. Supportive nurses were champions of any form of furthering one's education within the profession. Then there were the disgruntled, negative nurses who shared their disapproval of a young, inexperienced student even mentioning or dreaming of a career in anesthesia.

This was shocking and confusing initially, and, for a brief second, made me second-guess my decision to get on the path toward nurse anesthesia school. More than a few nurses would exclaim that too many people just wanted to go straight into anesthesia school without getting proper teaching and experience first. This made no logical sense to me, mainly because each school required at least a year of experience in an ICU prior to starting the anesthesia program. If the gatekeepers had already decided on an acceptable measure of experience, what level of experience did these nurses think I needed? I had expected to hear some pros and cons I might not otherwise have thought of about a profession, not a barrage of dissatisfaction about young nurses pursuing one of the most competitive and sought-after careers.

On one of my days with Debbie, I confided to her that I had made up my mind to pursue the nurse anesthesia route. As I had gone about asking for advice regarding the profession and the next steps to advance my career, I continually hit the same obstacle. No ICU wanted to hire a new graduate from nursing school, and especially not one who had already made up their mind to move on to anesthesia school when the opportunity presented itself.

Emory's nursing program had sheltered me from the realities of the profession and the workforce. Despite the interpersonal hurdles within the classroom, Emory, as an institution and university, invested in professors and programs that provided students with ample opportunities to be influential in the world around them and provided an open forum for facilitating and organizing networks that aligned personal career development and advancement with impactful actions on the health-care industry and the patients within it. It had never occurred to me that individuals would await us post-graduation who sought only to fully staff their day-to-day operations and had no intention of giving a temporary position to an ambitious new nurse who had no long-term commitment to the unit.

Coming from a culture that demanded development and expected leadership, this real-world experience was one of the first instances in which I saw what I believed was the nursing profession eating its young. Why would anyone not want to see a student progress? And why were these people the gatekeepers to the positions I needed? It seemed something had gone severely wrong in the system, and it was defeating me and many others like me before we ever got our start.

After I discussed this with Debbie, she again took a step out on a limb and introduced me to a close colleague of hers who not only became a major supporter but helped open the door for me by taking a chance with an unwritten contract. Debbie introduced me to Liz Casey, the nurse manager of the cardiovascular intensive care unit (CVICU) at the exact same facility where I was doing my maternity and pregnancy clinical rotation. After one of our surgeries for the day, Debbie walked me over to the recovery area, found Liz, and explained my plans and aspirations.

Without hesitation, Liz said, "Well, if Debbie believes in you, then this is what I can offer. If you are willing to come in and work as a paid nurse extern/nursing assistant for the next year, prove your dedication as a learner and team player, then I'll gladly hold a spot for you upon graduation and passing boards, and you'll have a home here on our unit."

I didn't know what to say. I was ecstatic, nervous, relieved, and amazed that someone would extend a helping hand without much a confirmation of skill set or knowledge. It was refreshing to have someone take a chance after having experienced so many closed doors in the same pursuit. Liz instantly began to start the hiring process, asking my availability and working me into the nursing schedule weekly.

Students were strongly discouraged from working while attending classes during the fall and spring semesters. But that was a state of mind I could never commit to. Having been employed constantly since I was fourteen years old, I was not accustomed to the luxury of not working, nor could I afford it. The new job afforded me financial benefits and a foot in the door to solidify my position post-graduation. Shortly after the introduction and paperwork were cleared, I quit my other nursing assistant job, which I had started as a junior in college upon beginning my semester as a nursing student. It was a job I was fortunate enough to be introduced to by Fern, who happened to be working in the human resources department of the hospital part-time. It was a job she had had since high school and one that she continued to maintain into our years in college. With her privileged knowledge of a pending job opening coupled with her introduction to the nurse manager of the telemetry department, I was offered a position within a couple weeks of attending my first class at Emory University. I worked 20 hours a week as a nursing assistant on a telemetry unit at the Dekalb Medical Center in Decatur, GA. After transitioning out of this position, I spent thirty-plus hours working weekly at the CVI-

CU as a nursing extern. I would work Friday evenings from 3 p.m. until 11 p.m., take a brief nap at home, and return the following day to do my 7 a.m. until 7 p.m. shift on Saturday and Sunday. Then it was back to attending classes on Monday.

This became my routine until I graduated and passed my boards in June of 2006. From there, I came on staff as a full-time registered nurse for the CVICU. Debbie and Liz will always have a special place in my heart for their role in my development and growth as a nurse anesthetist. Without their influence, risk-taking, and offering me a chance to prove myself, I would not have accomplished my goals in the accelerated timeline I did.

I spent the next six months working twelve-hour night shifts because that was the only one available to me. I used every day to learn and develop my instincts while practicing nursing care for patients' post-lung resection surgery, open-heart surgery, and valve replacement surgery. During that time, I got to see many types of patients. Most recovered, but there were also those who did not, which helped me learn to cope with death and to communicate compassion and understanding to patients and their families during these moments of anguish. All of these experiences, along with the critical and acute care of high-acuity patients, helped prepare me for what would be my first round of applications in the nurse anesthesia program. (High-acuity patients suffered from numerous co-morbidities and life-threatening diseases that required various medical interventions and medication modalities to optimize their physiology. This would include respiratory ventilators and vasoactive, cardiovascular infusions such as norepinephrine, epinephrine, milrinone, or dopamine.)

In January of 2007, just six months after my initial success on the National Council Licensure Examination (NCLEX, which is the national standardized test a graduating nursing student must pass in order to obtain a registered nurse license) and my subsequent hiring as a staff RN on the CVICU, I made the first round of application deadlines for anesthesia programs. I studied and took the GRE, which was a requirement for applicants at a number of the anesthesia programs across the country.

But my confidence about getting into a program on the first round of applications was not strong. It was a toss-up in my mind. So I kept my options open. Emory was starting a new acute care nurse practitioner master's program that specialized in emergency care. It was a yearlong program I thought would be interesting to take and gain more knowledge, and to create an even stronger application. Over the summer, following my success on the NCLEX, I applied to the emergency nurse practitioner (ENP) program and was accepted.

Over the course of six weeks, I weighed the option of attending school for another "fill-in" degree, which would mean more student loans, or focusing my attention on nurse anesthesia and the application process that lay ahead. I had to consider if it would be worth my time, energy, and money to get another degree I ultimately knew was not my end goal, even if it would be a stat booster coupled with more knowledge. At the time, the ENP career had not been fully established, and I didn't want the extra time and energy I would have to spend to interfere with my goals. I decided to forfeit my spot in the upcoming class at Emory and not apply for medical school. Instead, I tried my chances at applying to anesthesia programs across the country with deadlines upcoming in January 2007. I had about four months to polish my applications and to write all the required personal statements and essays for each application.

I knew it was a long shot to apply as a new graduate with merely six months of RN experience in a field that outlines in every application and on every resource that one year of critical care experience is required of all students if they're to be considered a viable applicant. Despite all the black-and-white text, I convinced myself that I was qualified, at least technically, to apply for the position. What would I lose by applying? Only an application fee. What harm would there be in being denied admission when I was knowingly taking a chance by even applying this early in my career? On the other hand, I had everything to gain in the event that some admissions office did see something in me that warranted taking a chance and offered me a position. I mean, after all, I am smart, black, and a male with the backing of Emory University, as Debbie reminded me. I felt I had shown myself to be a strong leader and proven my dedication as a student leader and committee leader through my short stint as a RN at the hospital. If nothing else, at least I would have the trial-and-error experience of having gone through the admissions process.

In my head, I had deciphered the text regarding experience to my own benefit. The mind is a powerful thing when you need and when you don't need to believe something. I just told myself that I'd worked on the same unit gaining weekly experience as an apprentice for more than a year prior to my graduation, and by the time classes actually started, which would be the following January following the application deadlines, I'd have at least one-and-one-half years of experience under my belt. Thus, I'd meet the established requirements of the academic institution as outlined in their catalogues.

I sent out five applications that winter, and I went on with my normal routines. I was halfway not expecting to hear anything worth noting regarding any of my applications. But, in the back of my mind, I was confident that I was the model student any school would love to get their hands on. Slowly, over the course of about five months, the letters trickled in. I really began to think I had a chance. First on the list was the University of Pennsylvania, which declined me as a first-time applicant, and I believe, with no evidence of course, that they turn away all first-time applicants to see how dedicated you are to the program. Just one of those things I told myself to soften the disappointment. Next came the interview offer from University of

Tennessee Knoxville (UTK), which I applied to more as a lifelong fan of football at the university than anything else. I thought this would be the perfect chance for me to go to anesthesia school while swimming in the sea of orange I'd always dreamed about. Along with the UTK interview offer came interview offers from Barry University in Miami and Samford University in Birmingham. But there was one school left, and it was the one school I had previously refused to apply to in undergrad because I was dying to leave my hometown: the University of Tennessee at Chattanooga (UTC).

In the meantime, I prepped myself for the upcoming interviews. I hyped myself up like I was Michael Jordan entering game seven of an NBA championship. I didn't have any resources to turn to, no mentor or former applicant I could readily call upon to give me a mock interview or anything of the sort. I didn't have an email address or phone number for a person I could reach out to for guidance along the journey because there were so few nurse anesthetists in my community or surrounding communities. I knew absolutely no nurse anesthetist of color prior to starting school, and not even until midway through my graduate program did I encounter another black CRNA, in clinicals.

I was left to my own preparation, and I went back to the same tactics that had helped me succeed in sports, and that was visualization and music. Routinely, during the days before the interviews, I would randomly catch myself listening to my favorite hip-hop songs and simultaneously telling myself how I was the shit and these programs not only wanted me, they actually needed me to make their program stand out. This was the kind of confidence you can't always say out loud for fear people might think you're an arrogant, narcissistic animal. But they were the words of affirmation I needed to get me over the hurdle because I had no one with whom to discuss the process. I had lost contact with both Debbie and Liz through a series of job transfers and relocations being that many networking companies had yet to become household names nor standards of the industry. Facebook was still in its infancy with users only being allowed who could provide their college or universities email addresses and LinkedIn was merely two years old.

In that very moment, I decided that if I ever made it through, I would have to be a part of disrupting that system for the better by helping future professionals pursuing the CRNA route. Many future practitioners would be more than great contributors to our profession if only they had access to resources and mentors who could help polish their approach. I had been in negotiations and business deals before, so I was fairly confident about how to carry myself during an interview. But I had no idea what to expect exactly, so I just did what I knew. I dressed nicely, smiled, showed charisma, carried myself with confidence, and answered questions truthfully.

The first interview was at Barry University. I was interviewed in a group setting with a roundtable of other highly qualified applicants. One by one, we were asked to explain who we were, our backgrounds, and why we chose the university.

What the hell! Who the hell has the luxury of picking the school they apply to based on characteristics or values of the school itself?

I'd never thought to research the mission of the school or the specialties they might offer; all I knew was their location, that they offered a nurse anesthesia program, and their application deadline was within the same timeframe as the other universities to which I was applying. Luckily, I was number five or so at the table, which gave the interviewers time to hear a few bullshit answers prior to mine.

My answer wasn't great, but it was partially honest. I said, "I chose Barry because it was on my short list of top schools within the Southern region where I am looking to attend school."

It was true that most all the schools I applied to were in the South. But whether Barry was rated as a top-tier school, I had no idea. It sounded good to me, so I went with it. The rest of the interview went as expected, with a few clinical questions and some personal questions as well.

After having experienced this interview, I felt more confident about attending my other interviews at UTK and Samford. UTK came and went just as quickly as spring rain. As I drove up to the interview, I was struck by something that seemed strange. I felt oddly out of place. I finally realized that there were no other faces like mine at these interviews. In Miami, the feeling didn't come across as much because there were people of color in the city and among the staff and a couple of other interviewers and applicants. But when I went to the UTK interview, this was vastly different. I wasn't seeing anyone of color within the immediate proximity of the interview. I may have had blinders on previously, but something about this trip awakened my senses to reality. I went ahead with the interview and everything went well, but I did fell like an outsider, with ninety percent of my interview pool from around Knoxville and the greater Tennessee area.

I had no idea what to expect from Samford. This little-known private Christian school in the heart of Alabama had barely crossed my radar. Even though one of my best friends, Louis, had started his undergraduate life there for a few semesters, it didn't register that this school had the potential to be my place of learning, achieving, failure, and redemption. The interview experience, from the outside, looked similar to that of UTK in applicant field and demographics, but there was something different about it all. I was fully expecting a more peculiar atmosphere and maybe expecting to not feel at home in the city of Birmingham based on its civil rights history. As a black man, I found it difficult not to be tense when walking into an interview at a conservative, small, Christian school within the South, in the same state that produced the likes of George Wallace and church bombings.

I wasn't foreign to the missions and guiding principles of Christian academic institutions, but Samford was different. There was no mistaking the role religion, and specifically Christianity, would play in the lives of students and faculty alike. All that said, I felt an inviting sense of honesty, compassion, friendliness, and genuineness from staff and faculty as soon as I walked through the doors to be escorted to the interview sessions. Plenty of schools go out of the way to create these appearances. Then, once you dive behind the scenes, you realize the horrors that awaited you.

I met a number of faculty during one-on-one sessions, but there was one who stood out to me: Dr. Theresa Culpepper. Dr. Culpepper was a warm spirit and soul from the moment I first met her. She greeted me with the embrace and compassion of a grandmother or great-aunt, with all of the expectations of achievement but with the nurturing gestures you can find only at home. With nearly forty years of experience, she was full of anecdotes and understanding for the path that lay ahead, but she was also sure to remind us that, just as others had survived anesthesia programs, so would we. During our interview, fate must have been shining on my side. As luck would have it, Dr. Culpepper was very familiar with my current place of employment in Atlanta as well as the cardiothoracic surgeons and cardiologist I worked with daily. It was on that note that we first bonded, over stories of people's old habits that had never changed and the new devices and structures of the ever-expanding Emory Hospital. This common ground helped to alleviate my nerves during the interview so that even though we were discussing critical care and physiological dynamics, it felt like any normal conversation with a colleague or old friend.

Dr. Culpepper was one of the only interviewers who directly and openly addressed my critical care nursing experience. She knew it had been less than a year for me post-licensure and decided to dive deeper to get an understanding of my path into the ICU. I explained that I was hired to work as a nurse extern and nursing aide while attending nursing school with the agreement that, immediately upon graduation, I would be hired as a nurse on the same CVICU unit where I had been an extern. I explained that I did this for two years prior to graduating and passing the NCLEX, and during that last eight months before graduation, I transferred into a full-extern residency program of sorts. I went on to explain how Liz had decided that I should begin to work side by side with the nurses, applying my clinical skills and learning on the job as I neared completion of my program. I confidently explained that because of this exposure, I had been submerged in waveforms and physiology and invasive monitoring and ventilator apparatuses for nearly three years. Dr. Culpepper acknowledged that by the time the program actually started, I would have officially met the requirement of one year of critical care experience. I felt like she wanted me to succeed just as much I did, and that gave me hope that there were people in this field with compassion and understanding. That fifteen-minute experience made me know this profession was right for me and the Samford program was the type of environment and culture I could gladly call home.

A few weeks later, it was time for the letters to be released, and I felt my heart pumping hard every time I went to the mailbox in anticipation of any official letterhead. They began to come in. I remember getting my first acceptance letter from Barry. I was ecstatic. It confirmed that no matter what, I was going to be in an anesthesia program the following year. Next came the less-than-pleasant letters. I was hoping to have multiple options to choose among because of the higher cost of living in Miami. But I received a rejection letter from the University of Pennsylvania. It wasn't surprising, seeing that I had not gotten any response prior to this one regarding an interview. I figured, rightly or not, that they were not willing to accept my experience for what it was at the time. So I just laid it on the desk at home as a reminder that rejection is possible, but so is success.

About a month later, I got the letter I had been waiting for from the Ida Moffett Samford University School of Nursing. I took a few days to weigh my options on which location and institution would be the best fit for me. I could not ignore the warm and inviting feeling of Samford and the conversation I had with Dr. Culpepper. After pricing the cost of living in Miami, the clear choice was Samford. I sent in my deposit and acceptance letter and began to prepare myself for the journey ahead in Birmingham.

CHAPTER 9:
SAMFORD UNIVERSITY
ANESTHESIA SCHOOL

"Sometimes in the professional environment, the old school is not ready for newer, more diverse and trendy students. At Samford, they weren't used to seeing a young African American man in this role, and certainly not with an earring. I don't think Donté sold out from who he is. He was always prepared and kind of let his education and abilities speak for themselves. Because he cares about people, he seeks to serve them well, and in serving them well, I think people see he's the real deal. I have seven kids. Two are African American males, and I'm about as lily white as they come. I show my kids Donté, my black kids and white kids. Show them that he's cool, hip, fun, intelligent, works hard, and cares about people. I'm so thankful to be able to do that." – Amy Snow, my clinical director

Even though I was an incoming student at Samford, I wanted to do my best to maintain my entertainment consulting obligations and to work my thirty-plus hours by driving back to Atlanta on the weekends. I saw myself flourishing in every aspect of my life and career while building the foundation to pivot my ambitions toward healthcare. But, to do this, I had to maintain a very stringent schedule to ensure there was no wasted time when classes were in session during the week.

Jumping into anesthesia school was every bit as challenging and overwhelming as everyone had warned. Three-hour-long, back-to-back classes were followed by a variety of labs and obligations, and were separated by thirty minutes of time to devour whatever likeness of food presented itself in the cafeteria. Classes would usually finish around 5:00 p.m., and after that I would take an hour break to have dinner in the university cafeteria. By 6:00 p.m., I was relegated to what became my third home, aside from my apartment and the anesthesia classrooms: the library. I was a pillar of the second-floor study desks and private rooms for five hours every night, or until the librarians would tell us it was time to lock up. My success at school and the continuation of my other endeavors depended on this stringent schedule.

There was never any other time in my career or academic studies when so much was demanded of me in the way of medical and scientific knowledge. The readings were one hundred pages or more a night, and they featured cadavers with specific nerves, muscles, bones, tendons, and ligaments we were all expected to recognize and label correctly on sight. It was far more than I had ever imagined.

The one highlight for me during this time was the examination format. As you may recall, I was a poor test-taker at the beginning of my undergraduate nursing program. I had not yet learned the proper way to take the nursing tests. The tests are given in a manner to force you to choose answers based on prioritizing as well as decide between "best-option" multiple-choice questions, and these type of tests haunted me for my first two semesters. Nurse anesthesia school was far better. Even with the abundance of material we were expected to master on a daily basis, tests were based on direct, qualitative results. There was only one answer for each question, no prioritizing involved. What you studied, read, researched, and learned was exactly what you were expected to know. This new form of testing and studying was refreshing. Throughout that first year, I was feeling like my best self. I must admit I felt a bit invincible. Not only had I graduated from one of the country's premier secondary schools for boys, but I had also succeeded at a top-tier undergraduate institution, successfully participated in owning my own business, and been admitted into one of the most highly competitive nursing specialties, and all of that by the age of twenty-three. I had a notable reputation in my circle in Atlanta, as well as in my larger network of classmates and colleagues, as someone who was definitely going places and going to have an impact on the community sooner rather than later.

Given my accolades and work ethic, I knew I had what it took to succeed in a nurse anesthesia program. I even knew that Samford was the right choice of school. But there was still something else that made me believe I had to be the best. It was like a light was shining on me to prove that I had what it took to succeed. I can say the pressure was not pushed on me from the staff or the faculty but by the lack of faces like mine. There was nowhere to hide. Not only was I one of the youngest members of my class, but I was also the only black male in a class of nineteen.

No amount of acceptance or inclusivity can deny the obvious scene that being different generates. I was the flashy yet intelligent, free-spirited Southerner making his way from the big city of Atlanta. And I was searching to find my place in the previously segregated city of Birmingham, home of the domestic terrorist attack on the 16th Street Baptist Church in the 1960s that took the lives of five little girls. It was 2008, and the Southern city was struggling with its identity in the world of a newly elected black president, President Barack Obama. The tension was felt. When the walls of the university did not protect me, the pressure was very present.

During my first year in Birmingham, I found out one of my close friends, Louis from McCallie, was living in the city as well. We would meet up with one another and go out for drinks and dinners. He allowed me the space and acceptance to really be myself and to express my true identity without judgment. He responded with the sincere empathy I needed. For months, I would go to school during the week and occasionally catch a happy hour with Louis. Then I'd drive to Atlanta to spend the weekend working in the Emory Crawford Long Cardiovascular ICU where I had worked before Samford.

Louis and I eventually decided to become roommates. He was a close friend who was my ear when I needed to vent. But he was also a needed ally. As a white man, he also knew the importance of supporting me and making sure people treated me no differently than they would him.

One occasion in particular stands out in my mind. Before moving in together, I would hang out with Louis and some of his friends and roommates from time to time. On one occasion when I was visiting, one of Louis's old roommates used the word *nigger* to describe someone he had had encountered. Louis immediately confronted him physically and verbally to let him know that wasn't a word to ever be used in his presence or mine. The old roommate knew as soon as it left his lips that he had made a huge mistake. But there were some cultural differences that underlined the guy's comfort using the term so blatantly and nonchalantly. He was South African, and I was aware of the cultural and historical complexities of apartheid and color division that likely influenced his choice of terminology. But Louis assured him there were no excuses. After Louis finished disciplining him, he made sure the guy came to me to apologize face-to-face.

I have had a number of white friends, classmates, professors, and colleagues support me and my endeavors. I know they believe in me. But, up until that moment, I had never had someone react so viscerally and emphatically on my behalf. This moment made me understand how white civil rights activists must have felt and reacted during their encounters with racists during marches and speeches. It was a turning point in my life. I instantly understood that true social justice and civil change has to include allies like Louis; it is the true embodiment of the American institution. As the historically perceived majority, the straight white man has played and will continue to play an important role in the transformation of opportunities and the destruction of stereotypes of minorities.

Louis has been and continues to be an ally, showing compassion, loyalty, and devotion. Even when a holiday vacation almost cost me everything.

CHAPTER 10:
CRIMINAL JUSTICE CRASH COURSE

"I was connected to Donté through the Emory Adopt-A-Scholar program. When we first met, it was one morning after Donté had been working all night. We sat and talked, and from then on it was like he was just part of our family. When Donté needed help, if I could be there, I was. When my grandson was getting ready to graduate from college, we'd given him money every year since he was a baby. I didn't know what else to give him. So I asked Donté, and he said to give him a passport. He said, 'you don't know what the rest of the world is like until you've seen it.' Donté used to take his backpack and just go somewhere by himself. And he always learned from those trips. I could not be prouder of him. And I love him."– Barbara Reed, my mentor

Weekends were often my escape from the rigidity of my routine. I could drive back to Atlanta and get some wind under my wings from my entrepreneurial work. To celebrate Labor Day 2008, I decided to take advantage of the long weekend by spending some time at a winery outside of Atlanta. My first year at Samford was almost over, and relaxation was much needed. I spent the day tasting wine, then that night I had dinner and libations. As the night was growing to a close, I somehow thought it was a good idea to drive the thirty-plus miles into the city of Atlanta to attend a party of an acquaintance of mine. To culminate the existing series of poor decisions that night, I also decided to drive back out to the winery around 3:00 a.m. En route, I was pulled over for speeding.

After failing a field sobriety test, I was arrested and taken to jail on suspicion of driving under the influence (DUI). My blood alcohol content was more than double the state limit, and I had no one to blame but myself. I spent that night in the Gwinnett County Jail's holding cell along with fifteen other unconvicted individuals. I completely sobered up once the cell door closed behind me. Cold, bristling air circulated throughout the jail. There was no space for comfort in the vast room among steel benches, one steel toilet, and one steel sink. Instantly, I felt the inhumanity of our justice system. My body and dignity were no longer mine. My clothes were stripped, including my shoestrings, belt, and tie. With my one phone called, I contacted Gilles Walter, my close friend, business partner, and an aspiring attorney in Atlanta, to make arrangements for my $3,000 bond.

I was released the next morning around 10:00 a.m. to find that my car had been towed and my Georgia license temporarily suspended until my hearing in a few weeks. This was the beginning of my year-long ordeal and self-inflicted nightmare with the criminal justice system, and of my crash course in understanding the problems facing so many people once they enter it. You are not meant to get free, or at least not without losing some part of yourself in the process. After being released and getting my car out of the impound, I returned to Birmingham to process my arrest and deal with the repercussions that could follow. When I got settled, the first thing I did was call my beloved mentor and adopted grandmother, Barbara Reed.

I was introduced to Barbara in the late spring of 2005 while a junior in nursing school. One day, while I was cleaning the lab at the nursing school, I was approached by one of the lead staff within the administration department regarding a potential scholarship opportunity. Somehow, my name had come up as a potential scholarship applicant for a new gift-giving vehicle. Barbara and her father had teamed up to become the first donors to the new project, and I had been chosen as their first recipient.

After spending two years at Mercer University at the request of her father, Barbara enrolled and became a 1957 graduate of Emory

School of Nursing as well as a graduate of the master's in nursing program in 1979. She was married to Robert Reed while a student in the nursing program and has remained a pillar of the Emory nursing community ever since. As a geriatric nurse practitioner, Barbara was a clinical faculty member at Emory through the 1980s and 1990s while also serving as a clinical specialist with a concentration in pain management. As the recipient of the Adopt-A-Scholar award, a $2,500 annual scholarship for my junior and senior year of undergrad, I had the pleasure of meeting Barbara over lunch one spring afternoon in 2005.

We instantly had a connection as we talked about our Southern roots, families, and respective experiences growing up in less-than-privileged circumstances. Since that first meeting, she has always been a staunch supporter and believer in not only my academic success but also in my impact within the profession as a whole. At the time, she knew I was working multiple jobs in order to make ends meet. But she was also compassionate about my goal of achieving an advanced degree.

So, during the rest of my time at Emory, we would meet three times a year for lunch or dinner at her home with her husband, family, and/or friends. She was always a warm spirit who gave me advice and encouragement in broad areas within my life, from career choices to relationship anecdotes to moral expectations. When Barbara's father, Mr. A. L. Alford, died at the age of ninety-seven, I made it a point to pay my respects to the family at the funeral.

Our relationship has developed over the years to the point where Barbara has even weighed in on my choice of companions, and, luckily for me, she has never led me wrong. As an advocate and member of the alumni boards and committees alike, Barbara has always ensured that I had every opportunity possible to be a part of the Emory community. She set the bar high for me in whatever way possible, near and far. I've had the opportunity to participate in and see the lasting impact alums can have within the growing Emory community, and that has always stuck with me; I will continually donate time, energy, and money to all of the institutions that have shaped me.

To my surprise, Barbara completely empathized with me after my arrest. As I came to her with my tail between my legs, she spoke words of encouragement, passion, and belief in me. She told me that this moment would not define me, and it would not be a roadblock ending my path. She told me that the success we had discussed and worked so hard to achieve was still mine for the taking. When she stepped up to assist me with my legal woes, without judgment and without a second thought, I knew her role in my life went deeper than merely donor and scholar. Barbara was integral to the team of people who helped rebuild and renovate Donté Flanagan.

There I was, twenty-four years old, a fixture in my nurse anesthesia program, and I was hiring an out-of-state attorney to prepare me to go before a judge. I was up against potential fines, probation, and jail time. I could not have seen this coming, so I struggled to find the words to break the news to my school's departmental director. I knew it could affect my standing within the university, given its strict devotion to Christian values, and its various bylaws.

I scheduled a closed-door meeting with my nurse anesthesia director, Dr. Mary Karlet. I gave her all of the details of my arrest and the pending court appearances and the possible repercussions. To my surprise, Dr. Karlet was very objective and deliberate in her response, as she stated she would share the details of my arrest with all parties who needed to know and give me specific courses of actions to take to stay ahead of all of the potential backlash that could come as a result of the verdict.

One of the first things Samford asked me to do was write a letter to the Alabama Board of Nursing to inform them of my arrest as well as contact the malpractice insurer for our student malpractice insurance to make sure that they would not drop coverage post-arrest. The board held the rest of my student nurse anesthesia journey in its hands. If the board decided to suspend my license or to offer some form of disciplinary action, I would not be able to attend clinicals until my punishment had been lifted, and the same went for the insurance coverage. Students are not allowed to participate in clinical activities if they are not covered by malpractice insurance. If my coverage was withdrawn or suspended, I would have to locate an insurance provider that would provide equivalent coverage at my own expense. The university and board decided to postpone any actions pending judgment on the actual court case.

I was relieved, but this was only the beginning. I wrote letters for documentation purposes to my director and started the waiting period for court appearances. Things at this point were busy and stressful, but mainly due to the lack of knowing what was coming next. The court dates were weeks away, and I was still attending class and working in Atlanta on the weekends. I had an Alabama driver's license by this point and was only driving to and from school and work. I had stopped going out and was becoming a subdued version of myself.

I was calling my attorney in Gwinnett County weekly to follow up on any correspondence coming from the court. Though we only had a handful of encounters, my experiences with one attorney served as one of the most important interactions of my twenties. Mr. Magarahan, as I called him, was known as the foremost DUI-DWI attorney in Gwinnett County and Georgia. He was stern and emphatic about my arrest and his expectations for me down the line. His direct attitude made for an easy relationship, but it also made me want to do my part in upholding the relationship.

As a veteran of the legal system and a peer of my mentor Barbara Reed, I'm certain he had forty years of legal experience by the time we met. He was a graduate of the University of Georgia at Athens and showed his Georgia Bulldogs pride throughout his office, from figurines and trophies to art and posters and many other forms of memorabilia. We did have light discussions on two things in which we had a common interest: bourbon and SEC football. He would give approval for enjoying libations coupled with the notion that it must be done responsibly. He didn't sugarcoat the facts. He told me straight up that I was a young black man with too much to lose, especially in a criminal justice system and a society that does not give handouts and is all too eager to knock a black man off the track to prosperity and keep him there.

I know there were probably countless unique scenarios he witnessed in his line of work, but I'm not sure how many of those encounters brought someone like my mentor, Barbara, a Southern white women in her seventies, into his office to pay the retainer fees for a young black man in his twenties: me. In our initial conversation, Mr. Magarahan made sure I understood that his services on my case would not be a handout. I immediately agreed to repay the legal fees to Barbara and the Reeds. The promissory note followed at our next meeting. It did make me gain respect for his practice as an attorney. These initial interactions allowed me to let down my guard and trust him, more than I had expected I would trust any attorney.

Out of my respect for Mr. Magarahan's time and my overall presentation of my case, I knew I could not afford to miss any court appearances. It took planning on my end to make sure I was available to travel the two-and-a-half hours back to Atlanta to make appearances. In the midst of all this, I'd get no special treatment that extended more time to me or delayed my school deadlines, assignments, and obligations. Dr. Karlet required and expected me to work extra hard to be an A student and not let my grades suffer. She also made it abundantly clear that I would not be receiving any additional time or extensions for assignments and projects beyond that of the law-abiding students. If I needed to complete an assignment early, arrangements would have to be made at the discretion of the professor for that class, including tests, papers, and presentations. The gift was that I was not immediately disciplined, at least not by my academic institution. They allowed the justice system to do that work instead. I am extremely grateful for that.

After months of delay, I finally had my court appearance and sentencing. Things got a lot more interesting and miserable after that. I thought going to jail was the most horrible and inhumane experience one could endure, but I found out being trapped in the justice system was even worse. A year after my court appearance, in April 2009, I pled guilty and received my sentence. In lieu of an extended jail sentence, I was ordered to serve one more day in a holding cell. In addition, I was ordered to complete forty hours of community service, undergo a psychological evaluation for alcoholism, complete a DUI defensive driving program, pay a $1,000 fine, and serve probation for one year. The probation also included suspension of my Alabama driver's license. Because of my lawyer's experience, we had completed most of these obligations prior to my sentencing, allowing me to focus on the probation requirements. They turned out to create one of the most strenuous six months I had ever experienced.

Within two weeks, I attended my probation appointment. I remember walking into that appointment at the Professional Probation Services Inc. office in Lawrenceville, Georgia, on May 6, 2009, and meeting my probation officer, Mrs. Glenn. She was a black woman and maybe five years my senior. She seemed to take interest in my wellbeing and my successful completion of the probation period. I was given all the parameters, opening my eyes to a world I never thought I would have to enter. Part of my probation included no illicit drugs, random drug screenings, no alcohol use, and no encounters with law enforcement that led to any form of citation.

Initially, I thought probation would be very simple, but as I began to examine my lifestyle, I knew that it was going to be a lot more difficult and risky than I had imagined. As an entrepreneur, I spent most weekends around alcohol and entertainment. Not only that, I had a history of parking and speeding tickets from Georgia, Alabama, and Florida. I was shocked to hear that any citation would be grounds for me being arrested and forced to finish my probationary period in jail.

Mrs. Glenn's instructions were coupled with encouraging words about being responsible and not careless. She emphasized the importance of making sure I refrained from alcohol and other unauthorized substances during my probation, especially during the weeks leading up to my probation visits. In our two short meetings, we got to discuss some of my goals and ventures, including my work as an event entrepreneur in Atlanta. I think she knew the event and party culture in Atlanta and wanted me to understand that it was up to me to follow the rules. Her compassion and down-to-earth responses and interactions helped to ease my anxiety and frustration with having to venture 150 miles from Birmingham every month to check in with her and to supply a urine sample. At least I knew she wasn't out to get me. Mrs. Glenn made our interactions feel less like punishment and ridicule and more like redemption and a means to an end.

When you're a part of the criminal justice system, accolades mean nothing and neither does your trajectory. None of that is on display when you're presented before a judge who is given the task of dishing out what they deem an appropriate sentence for the crime committed. It felt as if the probation period was a teaser toward freedom, and it was easy to see how young men and women spiral into traps similar to mine.

Given my list of fines and probation costs, I realized each task I needed to complete to satisfy the requirements of the probation would not be cheap. My psychology evaluation was $100, my criminal charge fine was $1,000, my DUI driving course was $350, and I had a monthly probation fee that included a drug screening that totaled $100 to $200 each visit. And that did not include my initial $3,000 bail, $100-per-hour lawyer rate, and hundreds of dollars in increased car insurance, car towing, and public transit. Not to mention I missed time from work and lost that pay. The bail and rehabilitation systems are not designed for citizens facing financial hardships or even mildly strained obligations to successfully manage and survive to become productive in society again.

I accepted my reality and began trying to navigate how to get my life back on track in the midst of these new restrictions. After my hearing, I assumed I had some flexibility that would allow me to manage the process with a restricted license that would allow me to travel back and forth between Birmingham and Atlanta. Little did I know; this was not the case. At the time, I had a Georgia driver's license, but I continued to travel between the two states.

But, not long after I had been placed on probation, I had another run-in with law enforcement following one of my events in Atlanta. I was driving home with my then-girlfriend, Jill, in Cobb County around 3:45 a.m. I remember being the only car on the road for a number of miles before I saw headlights. The car tailed my car for about two miles or so. Then the blue overhead lights came on. I pulled over. My heart was pumping as fast as ever as I relived the night of my DUI in my head. Despite this feeling, I hoped this would be a quick ten-minute interaction. I had become accustomed to having "routine checks" as a young black male in the South with a nice car; at the time, I drove a Hummer. I figured at this hour, this had to be a routine traffic stop. Boy, was I wrong.

The officer went through the usual protocol of asking me for my license and registration. He then asked where I was coming from and where I was going at this hour. I told him Jill and I had just left an event I hosted in the city and were headed home. Per my probation, I had not had any alcohol throughout the night, which gave me even more assurance that we would be back on our way in no time. After I gave the officer my license and registration, he disappeared into the darkness at the rear of the car to process his findings.

I could see him faintly in the rearview mirror as he scanned the license and began typing. After a few moments, I noticed that he was making a gesture as if speaking to someone two-way on his shoulder. This went on for what felt like fifteen minutes. At this point, my anxiety began to creep up. I explained to Jill that I didn't know what was going on, but it didn't look good. Another eternity of five or so minutes went by, and I noticed a second set of flashing lights pull up behind the initial officer's car. The officer returned, and I was asked to exit the vehicle and come to the back of the car. I instantly knew shit was about to hit the fan.

After stepping out of the Hummer, I walked around to the rear and asked the officer, "Is there a problem?"

He answered, "Well, you tell me. Is there a reason you're driving on a suspended license?"

My entire heart sank. But I tried to keep it cool and explain that there must be a mistake because I should have a special provision showing that I was allowed to go back and forth from work and school. He replied that no such exemption was present in the computer system.

And then it began all over again. He told me I'd be going to jail until I was able to pay bail and schedule a court date to resolve the issue. By this point, I knew how the next ten hours were going to play out, with a visit to booking and to a cell after being undressed and strip-searched. I gave Jill the rundown and told her to call Gilles to let him know what was going on. He knew how to start the process for bailing me out because he'd been here with me before. And so began a whole new set of charges.

After I was placed in the back of the police car, one of the officers drove us to the jail as I sat quietly in disbelief that this was happening again. Once we got to the jail, we stopped outside the intake department and sat in the car. I was wondering what was going on, and then I saw the two officers in the front pull out a three-inch book. It was a book of charges and procedures. They fanned through it, locating extra charges they deemed relatable to my situation. I asked why the other charges, and one officer told me, "It's not up to us to determine whether you're innocent or not. We enforce the laws as we see them. You can deal with the results with the court. That's your problem, not ours."

I was in disbelief. I couldn't believe what I was hearing. I knew I was at the mercy of the courts at this point. No amount of conversation or explanation was going to change what was being written on my record. So there I was, back in a cell with four new charges, any one of which could be seen as a violation of my probation, and that could mean the subsequent punishment of having to spend the remainder of my sentence behind bars for six to twelve months.

Having had to sit within the holding cell before, I knew to expect the lengthy processing steps that would see me caged for at least ten hours and possibly two days, given that it was a holiday weekend. This time I was completely sober behind bars. I was in a holding cell by myself for the duration of the day. The solitude and time alone made me contemplate what I valued most in life, and my fate. I knew the moment I left that cell, the real work and stress would begin, all over again. How was I going to get to and from work across state lines? How was I going to get to and from class? How was I going to get to clinicals?

After spending the better part of ten hours at the Cobb County Adult Detention Facility, I was finally released on bail. I was elated to be allowed to be processed the following day as opposed to having to wait until the following business day. Jill met me just outside, and the first call I made was to the office of my lawyer, Mr. Magarahan. For a second time, I had to discuss an arrest case. But, because it was the holiday weekend, I was forced to leave a voicemail and sit in anticipation for three more days before he returned my phone call.

Mr. Magarahan again scheduled a time to meet with me, and within a week we started the process all over again. We located the details of the arrest, pending charges, and information regarding my future court appearance. This case for my lawyer came with a new bill for me. And the icing on the cake was that I was actually charged for two cases because the arrest would call for two criminal defenses and appearances, one for the probation violation and another for the citations and arrest in Cobb County.

It seemed that just when I thought I had things under control, my freedom was costing me more and more. I wasn't scheduled to meet with my probation officer for about three weeks, which was more than enough time for her to be notified of my arrest. As if things couldn't help but get worse, I also received a new probation officer. Mrs. Amaya replaced Mrs. Glenn. They were completely opposite of each other. Mrs. Amaya was a twenty-something petite white lady who was very matter-of-fact. She avoided eye contact with me and was very short and direct when it came to my requirements.

If there was any feeling of compassion or belief in redemption, I neither saw nor felt it in our brief interactions. Mrs. Amaya gave off the impression that she was there to follow through with the enforcement of the justice system. There was no talk of my background, goals, or aspirations. She was new to the position, and maybe this stoic demeanor was a way to create a barrier that prevented clients from trying to take advantage of her or miscalculating her stature for weakness or being a pushover. Regardless of the reason, our lack of personal connection reminded me that I was a number, just another piece of paper for her to push through for the day.

When I went before my presiding judge again, he was at full liberty to sentence me to mandatory time in jail for violating probation. A lot of this sentencing was based on the recommendation of my probation officer, which I was leaving my attorney, with his expertise, to handle. But deep down, I just knew for sure that Mrs. Amaya was gunning for the harshest of punishments for me. I was at a standstill. It could go either way. The days leading up to my court date were more stressful than ever because I could not get a grasp on which way my probation officer was leaning and or get any confirmation from my lawyer as to what to expect. He was actually calmer than I thought the circumstances warranted. But with him having decades of experience in the matter, I assumed he felt confident that it would all be just fine. Easy to say when it's not *your* life and career on the line.

The day came, and I still didn't know for certain what was about to happen. I put on my best business suit and took out my earrings, a gesture I was told by Mr. Magarahan would better present me to this judge, The Honorable John F. Doran, Jr. I met my destiny alongside my probation officer at one table and my lawyer at another. Little did I know, in a last-minute meeting between the two of them, a deal of leniency was made on my behalf because I had met all prior obligations of my sentencing and not had any prior arrest history. Judge Doran allowed me to continue on my current sentencing path without further punishment. But he did explicitly state that there would be no more passes given out for missteps along the way and confirmed that I was not allowed to operate a vehicle in any form or fashion until all of the obligations of my sentencing and probation had been met and approved by the courts. Whew! I had dodged a bullet.

At least under the jurisdiction of Gwinnett County. There was still the matter of the second arrest that had occurred in Cobb County. I still had to go to traffic court. Things began to blur together, as I was in a state of survival at this point. Not only was I still having to make court appearances and probation meetings while being careful to stay out of trouble, I was also having to navigate life between school, clinicals, and work, a map of which would cover a distance of 160 to 250 miles one way. I had to maintain my poise and sanity and perform without mistakes amidst all of the chaos. Because of my new probation requirements, I was riding a Greyhound bus from Atlanta to Birmingham weekly to maintain the job that covered my legal fees. Preceptors needed to see me excel, and professors needed me to perform exceptionally on their exams. My whole journey was to prove that giving me some leverage was not a mistake, that I was more than worth the risks. But, because of that, I was free of excuses regarding the matter. It was my weight to carry and my problem to address daily.

Clinical assignments were given to students who lived near me so we could carpool to and from sites. One such clinical site was more than an hour away. By the blessing of God and the large hearts of my cohort, classmates agreed to pick me up in the morning and drive me to the clinical, where we bonded over the stress of the clinical and life. One classmate, Leah Deanhardt, knew my ordeal intimately and knew the price I was having to pay mentally, physically, and financially. It was a blessing to have her near, as her faith and optimism kept me pushing forward.

The hardest span came when I had to live out of a hotel while on a clinical rotation in Jackson, Alabama. It was about halfway between Birmingham and Atlanta. I would take the Greyhound bus and then walk or take a taxi from the train station to my hotel about a mile from the hospital. There was no funding allocated for such a clinical rotation and no housing provided, so I had to pay out of pocket for eight weeks of living. I was alone, away from friends and family. It was a period of solitude. I would spend $5 on a Little Caesar's large pizza each Monday and ration it to survive the rest of the week. On the days of clinicals, I would grab my anesthesia bag and books and walk to and from the hospital, no matter the weather. I made special arrangements with Greyhound, the taxi company, and the hotel because I was going to be a regular visitor for the near future. Small victories like that, along with my open credit card accounts, helped to make things seem bearable. I kept faith things were going to get better.

With the probation violation successfully behind me, it was now time for me to make the journey to Atlanta again to see what my fate would be concerning the charges in Cobb County. After countless prayers and weeks of anxiety, it was time for me to appear before yet another judge. This experience was much more relaxing and comforting than my other trips to court. Maybe it was the vast quantity of people who were present that made the process simpler, or maybe it was because I had already experienced so much of the process I had grown desensitized to it. Nonetheless, I saw some twenty to thirty people go ahead of me with much more drastic traffic violations. I got to see the lenience of the courts but also the quarter from which this judge drew his conclusions. He was much more of an equalizer than a true punisher, asking more in-depth questions and allowing the defendants to explain their charges and any efforts to rectify the problem. This gave me hope as my time neared and my lawyer arrived to stand with me before the judge. When our time came, we walked up to the table together and it began.

I spoke minimally, with simple "yes, sir" and "no, sir" responses. My attorney took the liberty to explain to the judge the circumstances surrounding the arrests and the charges. After explaining to the judge that we had also taken the matter to the courts of Gwinnett County and arranged a resolution with that jurisdiction, the judge was convinced that the matter was now a moot point. He acknowledged that failing to stay fully in one lane while driving at 3:00 a.m.

wasn't necessarily the most incomprehensible thing in the world. The judge was satisfied that the matter had been resolved as far as the other courts were concerned, and that my arrest and the aftermath of that morning were punishment enough. And with that, he dismissed the case!

Roughly $10,000 later, I was a free man. I would be living within the confines of probation, but at least I was allowed to go back to school and continue my education, even if it meant having to charge hotel stays and bus fares weekly. Jill was instrumental as a girlfriend and confidant during this time. I appreciated her spirit and willingness to support me mentally, emotionally, and physically as I went through my devastating arrest and sentencing. Together we coordinated transportation and lodging from Atlanta across Alabama to make sure I could successfully continue attending school, working, and attending my probation obligations. We successfully moved and lived as a unit, my family away from home.

As time went on, we both knew that our paths were destined to venture to different ends, but we respected each other. Jill was never going to leave Atlanta, and I was slowly but steadily outgrowing the city. Today, she holds a master's in healthcare administration, and I had the honor of writing her recommendation letter for her first job placement after graduation.

For the six months after my second court appearance, I stayed on the straight path with no deviations. My routine became one where I would call in favors from friends and classmates to help get me from point A to point B. Beyond that, my life was devoted to school and clinicals. I couldn't think of anything else but counting down to the moment when I got my true freedom back. I was always looking over my shoulder and tiptoeing around, as if at any moment I would be accused of breaking the law and the cycle would begin all over again. The smallest citation loomed over my head every single day, and I knew that so much as a jaywalking ticket could land me back behind bars for an unspecified amount of time. The freedoms and liberties many everyday citizens get to enjoy without fear of repercussions were now the difference between freedom and imprisonment for me.

The continuous stress and worry had effects on my psyche. One of these was how my values changed or merely solidified. Freedom instantly climbed to the top of my value list and has not been dethroned since. The freedom to have a sip of wine, look both ways and then cross the street, or make a mindless mistake like forgetting to turn on my blinker. The freedom to walk, drive, or fly. To know that I could not travel out of the country without permission was a different type of imprisonment. I lived these agonies daily for six months, with monthly visits to the probation office for my scheduled appointments and drug and alcohol urine testing.

Even at the end of it, my fate was still at the discretion of the judge. To my great relief, the judge saw my six-month timeline as adequate and accepted my request for early dismissal, having completed all of the requirements and having remained out of any further trouble. And, just like that, it was over.

CHAPTER 11:
US CAPITALISM 101

"A couple years after The Lawrence opened, we were concerned about street presence. We had been talking about a sign, where it was going, who was going to pay for it. And here Donté comes just walking in with a chalkboard sign. He doesn't make perfect the enemy of good. Donté has a get-it-done type of attitude. People always talk about work-life balance. His view is life-work balance. He has helped me to understand that we do what we love in our professions only to allow us to be able to do what we love in life. He's so comfortable in his skin that sometimes it's scary. But, that's also the thing that fuels him. He knows that the better he knows himself, the better he can relate to people. I think that's a family trait of ours. We're very much pleasers and social people." – Harvey "Trey" Daniels III, my cousin and business partner

I came off probation as I started my final semester at Samford. And it felt like the last semester just flew by. How could it not? I was liberated again. With my freedom reinstated, my burden was light now. During that time, I was allowed to do two of my final clinical rotations near Atlanta. One facility in Cartersville, Georgia, even supplied me with housing while I was in their clinicals. In divine intervention, God also blessed me with job offers from both locations, the other being North Fulton Hospital in Roswell, Georgia.

I decided to accept the offer from North Fulton. I had the guidance of one colleague who became a confidant. I shared with him my circumstances during the clinical rotation, and he advised me that the best approach for the rest of my professional life was to lead with the facts and the truth. Employers can either proceed and accept me, or not. But what they cannot overcome is a dishonest employee who begins the relationship without integrity. It was then that I started both a hard copy folder and electronic folder of all of my legal documents, including community service, defensive driving certifications, my psychological evaluation letter, and my communications with the various nursing boards. Now, I just attach the folder along with a prepopulated letter explaining my arrest and the resulting sentencing.

It felt like I was getting my life back on track. In May 2010, I graduated from Samford, and, at twenty-five, signed my first six-figure contract. Yes, the contract I mentioned at the beginning of this book. Now you have more perspective on why achieving this moment—in a field lacking in black men under circumstances typically stacked against black men—meant so much to me.

And still, all of that was just the preparation. Now that I was in the profession, I had to get the licensing exam. It took me three weeks of studying ten hours a day to prepare. Though I admit it was the hardest exam I've ever endured, then and now, I managed to pass it on the first attempt. I felt I had put all those negative experiences behind me. Almost two months to the day of passing the exam, I quit my staff nursing position in Atlanta and became an independent nurse anesthesia provider. From there, I chased every opportunity that came my way.

I also began seriously thinking about how to strategically ensure that all of my current and future entrepreneurial ventures would be sustainable. It had only been a couple of years since the 2008 financial collapse, known as The Great Recession. Atlanta was still reeling from the effects of that, with halted construction projects throughout the city. It was during this time that I had the opportunity to purchase my first two condos in the heart of the notable community of Buckhead. They were foreclosures, and I was able to turn them into rental incomes. In addition, another unforeseen opportunity presented itself. In 2012, my cousin, Harvey Daniels III, and I were offered the chance to partner in a restaurant in Midtown Atlanta. Trey, as I call him, and I didn't have any experience as restaurateurs. But we did have experience as hosts and managers within the restaurant industry. Throughout high school, Trey had worked his way up to manager at his local McDonald's, and I had played the role of a cashier at two different Wendy's as well as host at a Cracker Barrel.

I trust Trey. He is the youngest child of my maternal grandmother's brother, Harvey, making him my second cousin. Because of the years of separation between himself and his older siblings, Trey grew up like an only child in Decatur, Georgia, with his mother and father. Given his proximity to me in age, when he visited family over summers in Chattanooga, we spent most of our time together. Though he towered over us—he's now a staggering six foot five—Trey was always a gentle spirit. He's a fun and jovial soul who is Southern at heart but also a chameleon who can blend in any social circle. Because he lived in Atlanta growing up, I depended on Trey to bring me all the coolest sayings and clothing every summer so I could be ahead of everyone in Chattanooga. I looked to him for all things trendy, especially Southern rap because So So Def, Outkast, and the Dungeon Family were in his backyard.

Our summers were spent at the family house with huge, family-style meals every night. So you could say childhood was our first experience of hosting, serving, and curating fun experiences among groups of people. From block parties to fish fries, people came from all over the city to visit the house. We saw what good food could do to relationships. Trey went on to attend the HBCU Xavier University in New Orleans. One year older than me, he was the first of our generation to complete a bachelor's degree. He was also the first to introduce me to New Orleans when I visited him in college. Since moving to New Orleans in 2018, he has also been instrumental in developing my network in the city. Trey's career as a corporate attorney has moved him and his family from Atlanta to Sacramento,

California, and back again. He now resides in Alpharetta, Georgia, with his wife, daughter, and son.

Throughout our lives, Trey has set the bar. He has been an example of the achievement I always want to measure myself against. He went out of state for college, and so did I. He then pursued a graduate degree by attending law school at the University of Georgia, the same program as my attorney, Mr. Magarahan. I, in turn, went on to nurse anesthesia school. And so on.

Joining forces in Atlanta was almost inevitable. We knew the restaurant would be a legacy our family could enjoy for years to come. We also knew that our family hadn't been in this position, so the charge to break the cycle was heavy on our shoulders. We leveraged the fact that we were young and would still have the benefit of age on our side to bounce back from any losses we experienced during the process. So we decided to take the plunge and teamed up with an experienced Atlanta restaurateur. There we were, in our twenties and opening a laid-back, high-quality restaurant offering fresh farm-to-table dining and handcrafted cocktails. The restaurant is in an established neighborhood known for its critical approach to dining and immensely high standards for what belongs and does not belong inside the community.

For more than nine months, we battled the city for permits as well as the homeowners' association and neighborhood organizations for acceptance of our vision. We spent our evenings demolishing, rebuilding, hosting, cleaning, and serving patrons. Slowly, we were able to be less hands-on as the restaurant began to stand on its own. Seven years later, I'm proud to say our restaurant is still there, welcoming regulars, after various expansions and renovations and winning a number of local awards.

While opening the restaurant, I also began strategically shifting my event planning operations. I committed to doing four major events a year, with a couple of hip-hop shows sprinkled in the midst. By this time, I had already begun estate planning, meeting with financial advisors for guidance on retirement planning and insurance for my loved ones. The small-town black boy in Chattanooga still lived in me, and I truly believed in my heart I would be dead by thirty, like all the statistics told me. I was going to live life by taking advantage of every amazing opportunity that presented itself. But at the same time, I wanted to make sure my life and opportunity weren't for naught. I wanted to make sure that my family and the generations behind me had the financial security, backing, and opportunities that had not been afforded to me. If I was to leave a legacy, I wanted to leave Earth having blessed those behind me. I created living wills and strategically structured insurance policies and set up my businesses such that my family would be supported in the event of my demise.

With work under control, I had the opportunity to return to my love for travel; it was the ultimate freedom, my way to spread my wings and to dive within myself more. Twenty-six came, then twenty-seven, twenty-eight, and twenty-nine, and all of a sudden there I was. It was 2014, and I was edging closer to that pinnacle of thirty.

One of my best friends, Julie Nguyen, had asked me on multiple occasions what I wanted to do for the big day. Over and over, I told her I didn't know; I just had never thought the day would come, so I had never thought to plan anything in relation to it.

One day, I gave it some thought, and I finally told her I just wanted to sit on a mountain in nature and reflect. I envisioned a moment alone with my memories, God, and nature while I sat on a cliff. And so I told her, and being the friend she is and knowing the person I was, she blew my mind with a priceless suggestion that was both perfect and expected. She said, "Let's go back to Hawaii."

We had met up in Hawaii in the February following my graduation from Samford in 2011. I was at my first anesthesia conference as a

CRNA. And she was on the final leg of her homecoming tour of Southeast Asia after serving three years as a Peace Corps representative in Ghana. I've known Julie for more than two decades. We met through mutual friends at our respective private schools in Chattanooga. She attended the Catholic private school about a mile down the road from McCallie.

I believe that we gravitated to one another by being placed in these communities full of privilege that our families and we ourselves didn't know directly. We both had a hustle spirit within us that couldn't be taught, and we both had seen firsthand the hard work and dedication of our mothers, specifically, as they did everything they could to give us the life they didn't have. Julie is Vietnamese, so there was also this mutual respect and understanding as minorities. I can relate to her immigrant experience alongside the forced migrant experience of black people in America, especially the South.

Having been born in Los Angeles, Julie had a broader experience of culture that I learned from early on. We also fed off each other's cruel and misunderstood humor as well as our innate ability to stand out in a crowd. Throughout high school, we hung out at sporting events, friends' homes, and her mother's nail salon. Julie has always been a motivating voice telling me I can achieve anything and that I was already achieving greatness. She has a spirit that wishes everyone to be their best self and believes in equal treatment and respect for all people, especially the underrepresented and silenced. Julie is also one of the most brilliant, creative minds I've had the pleasure to witness. Since she left the Peace Corps, she's been a star branding manager and campaign manager for numerous businesses and projects. I also got to witness the experience of her joining the traditional black sorority, Delta Sigma Theta Sorority Inc.

We've been there for one another at our best and our worst, and we even went through the proverbial breakup that is the mark of any true friendship that will withstand the test of time. We know more secrets about one another than I could ever count. She's been directly and indirectly responsible for a number of my friendships and relationships. Julie also had the unfortunate opportunity to witness a number of my unsuccessful attempts at lust and love, but most notably she's the link between me and my future wife. I guess she knows me better than I know myself.

So, for thirty, I went to Hawaii with Julie, and we were hosted by some of her close friends from the Peace Corps. Little did I know that this emotional and spiritual vacation would be another pivotal point in my life. Our accommodations in Hawaii were supplied by Julie's former Peace Corps colleagues and by friends in Honolulu. We decided to climb Diamond Head mountain straightaway from the airport. I had the opportunity to take a deep breath and to embrace the vast nature around me, and I knew instantly that this trip was going to be nothing like any other I had taken. Along with the all the wonderful things that come with being shown a new city or country by local residents, I was blessed that my friends made a concerted effort to provide me with the solitude within nature that allowed me to reflect deeply on my life.

On my actual birthday, June 18, we made our way to an isolated beach, and I ventured away from the group for my own moment. That's when it all poured out of me. I cried and relived all of the ups and downs of my life. I truly felt the grace that God had showed me. At any number of moments, my life could have taken a totally different path. I recognized that many steps had to be aligned for me to get to that very particular moment. In that moment of reflection and thankfulness, I had a yearning to do more, to challenge myself further. More importantly, I knew I was destined for a larger story. I decided I was moving to New York City immediately. Not only was it an opportunity for me to challenge myself with a new city full of new obstacles, from transportation to weather to culture, it was also an opportunity to continue learning.

I decided that I had to go back to school to get my doctorate and I had to do it at an Ivy League school.

I chose Columbia University at that moment on a rock on the sandy beaches of Honolulu. I didn't know how, but I knew I was taking a plunge. One that I couldn't completely articulate to others without receiving some form of skepticism or confusion. The first person I told this to was Julie, and she was in total support of it, though I know she could hardly believe it at the time because I had never done anything so drastic. I had to do it, and not just for me, but for those who looked up to me. Growing up in Chattanooga, I had been totally enamored with getting out. To me, at that time, Atlanta was the promised land. And I'd made it there. Others in my community felt the same way, and I was someone they could relate to, so I had to keep showing them a picture of something more. I envisioned my nieces and nephews, and I just wanted to give them hope. I wanted them to have a dream, a vision beyond the image sports and music painted in our community.

After leaving the beach, I called my mother and told her the news, and she was speechless. Even though we had had a tumultuous relationship during my teens, we began to develop a stronger and different relationship following my transition to campus during my freshman year. After saying our goodbyes and watching her emotional response to leaving me to navigate that new phase in my life, she has continued to call or text me every night to say "good night and I love you." These interactions became even more important as I watched her navigate her inevitable divorce of my then-stepfather and venture back out into the world of dating again. My compassion, empathy, and understanding grew, and her love and trust in me as a man began to flourish.

On the other hand, however, she had grown comfortable with me being within a two-hour drive, but she never fathomed that I would ever wish to move nearly eight hundred miles away. As hard as it was to hear her shock, I knew that her reaction was the confirmation I needed that this was the right decision to make. I needed to also show *her* that my life, *our* lives, could and would be larger than the limited walls around us. I knew my mother believed in me; that was never in question.

But this exchange showed me that she hadn't envisioned me beyond where I was, and that was a sign of a bigger issue: the measure of being content. I had to show everyone what was possible.

CHAPTER 12:

COLUMBIA UNIVERSITY

"Donté is always the success story I reference in regards to the importance of exposing youth to new opportunities and broadening perspectives. I'm very proud of his growth and maturity over the years. He's definitely become less extra, in a good way. When we were younger, Donté had a tendency to do the most; he did everything to the max. Now, instead of doing things to gain notoriety, his actions are more centered around what will truly benefit him and bring him joy. He's become incredibly thoughtful about making better decisions for himself, his future family, and the legacy he wants to leave behind." – Julie Nguyen, my friend

When I got back home to Atlanta, I called my other close friends with the news. They were also shocked and largely in disbelief. They thought it would be just a temporary three-month venture. Never did they imagine that I would make this change a permanent relocation. Nonetheless, they supported me. I drafted my letter of resignation from my CRNA role in Atlanta, and I immediately began to plan how I would find tenants for my condo. I also applied for my state licensure in New York. A couple of weeks after my birthday trip, I took a vacation to New York City, where I crashed with Julie and her roommates, who lived in Brooklyn. Half-believing I was moving, they extended me an invitation to move in with them while I was establishing myself in New York. So, I had a couch to sleep on and a working plan for renting my Atlanta condo. The only thing keeping me from moving was a job.

Having no true understanding of the healthcare system within Manhattan or Brooklyn, I just scoured the internet for New York City CRNA positions. I cast out four applications, and something beyond belief happened. While on vacation, I wandered the city, trying to get the lay of the land. That Saturday, on a bus in Manhattan, I received a phone call. The call was from East Manhattan Anesthesia Partners, and they were interested in interviewing me. The anesthesia director on the other end of the call asked how soon could I fly up. I explained to him that, oddly enough, I was in the city at that very moment. To my astonishment, he asked if I would be willing to meet him and the other partners for an impromptu interview the following day. I said, "Of course!" I paused. Then, I added the disclaimer that I had only vacation clothes so I would not be wearing a suit and tie. To my surprise, he said it would not be a problem and agreed to meet with me.

Sunday morning arrived, and I couldn't believe it. I was making my way to Second Avenue and Fourteenth Street for the first time in my life, and I was doing it for a job interview in shorts and a T-shirt. That moment made me feel like New York City was going to be the type of place I would fit in and love. My mindset was already changing as I gained comfort in being my authentic self. In the interview, I explained my professional experience in trauma and labor and delivery, and my decision to drop everything and move up north. I left the interview still in shock that it had actually happened. I had no expectation that anything would come of it; I was just excited that people were actually receiving and reviewing my CV. To my surprise, it took all of two hours for my interview follow-up. Shortly after meeting up in SoHo with Ashlee Yates, a friend I was visiting, I got a call from the anesthesia director. He was calling to formally offer me a position as a staff CRNA. It was official; I would be working in Lower Manhattan. Four weeks from the day I vowed to move, it was confirmed. There was no looking back.

In September of 2014, I completed my move to New York City. I arranged to have my furniture and other belongings moved to a storage facility in Brooklyn. In dramatic fashion, I decided to give up my beloved Mercedes-Benz CLS 500 and sold it the day before I moved. Like many New York transplants, I was originally committed to keeping my car at all costs. I was convinced that I had worked too hard for it to part ways with it. But, after much back and forth with friends who advised against bringing my car north and personally calculating the enormous monthly cost, I decided to sell it. I spent my first three months in the city living on Julie's couch in the Brooklyn apartment she shared with two other roommates.

By December, I had finally managed to save up enough money to move into my own apartment in Bedford-Stuyvesant. My Christmas gift to myself was that apartment and its furnishings. The city was beginning to feel more like home. In the spring of 2015, I turned my sights to Columbia University. I had never applied to an Ivy League school. I'd always assumed I was an exceptional, grade-A type of student, but not one capable of fitting into the perfect world of the Ivy League experience. My view was jaded and completely false. When you're achieving at a noticeable level but still not number one, your psyche tells you you're good—just not *that* good. But more life experiences had convinced me to make the leap and strive for more.

I regularly try to explain why I chose to go back to school for my doctorate and why I chose Columbia. But it never quite resonates the way I want it to. I've learned that one experience I had is my best explanation. One day, while working in Manhattan, I found myself needing to dress in more businesslike attire for plans I had after work, so I chose to wear a pair of dress shoes into the operating room. My first encounter that morning was with a senior otolaryngologist and surgeon who I know had been practicing for at least a decade beyond me. He made a statement that told me he assumed his station in life was far beyond mine. He walked into our operating room, acknowledged me with a nod, and then gave our patient his attention during the induction process. Afterward, he asked, "Are those Ferragamos? Because I have some shoes like that. But they're Ferragamos."

What was the proper response to that? I had stopped wearing Ferragamos the year before when I discovered I enjoyed more durable, handmade shoes created by craftspeople. And there he was assuming that I, his staff person, could not be in a position to afford items similar to what he owned. I toyed with returning the male bravado or, better yet, coming at him as the black male with a chip on my shoulder. Or I could pretend the statement never happened. I chose to heed the words of the Bible verse tattooed on my shoulder from Proverbs 27:2, "Do not brag, do not boast, let another man speak highly of you."

I responded, "No, these aren't Ferragamos."

This is just one example of the various conflicts that have been presented to me as a black man both in privileged positions and exposed to others in them. No matter the situation, I, as a black man, have to weigh all of the options before I respond. I've learned to always confront such situations with confidence and authority while maintaining respect. That is why moving to New York wasn't enough. Working in New York wasn't enough. Earning my doctorate wasn't enough. It had to be Columbia. It's bigger than just my experience or success. Someone has to be the voice and image who shows those in less interactive experiences what is possible while shaking up the norms.

Columbia accepted me, and I was able to pursue my doctorate of nursing practice. Classes started August 2015, and I had never felt this kind of fear about succeeding. I was also crossing into a world I had never felt worthy to experience. I was one of a cohort of five, and my classmates were all from diverse backgrounds. But I was the only black man and the only one with a specialty in anesthesia. On this journey, there were limited ways to measure myself against my colleagues. Being an island of one forced me to start measuring my growth and success against my own goals and objectives. As I began to embrace my more authentic self and to live more aware, I began to see the benefits of my doctorate program.

Columbia is what's known as a city university because it is located in the center of a metropolitan landscape. It is surrounded by neighborhoods, subways, and commuters who are living their daily lives with no responsibility or interaction with the university, despite its proximity. As a student at the nursing college, I had online courses during the week and attended class once a week at the medical campus, which is about fifty blocks farther north in Manhattan than the main campus. This would not only mean that my commute to school would be an extra thirty to forty minutes, for a total of about one hour and fifteen minutes every Friday, but also that I was able to appreciate the more-diverse Hispanic community of Washington Heights.

I remember riding from Brooklyn to Columbia, and the commuter demographics changed at least three times during that trek across south Brooklyn, through the southern border of Manhattan, up through the west side of Lower Manhattan, and finally uptown. As I embarked on my journey in Bed-Stuy, I traveled with neighbors who were black, with sprinkles of white faces mixed in, but as we ventured nearer Manhattan and eventually into Lower and Midtown Manhattan, my commuting partners turned more white and less black and brown. The landscape and population of the city changed right before my eyes from stop to stop. About halfway up the island, there's another color and cultural shift from black to white to brown.

I had never been in such a diverse community of people of color. It made me smile and lifted my heart every time I got to see the families and the children bustling through their routines. It was a micro-community where people of color dominated the culture of the neighborhood, despite Columbia being there. That giant institution still couldn't penetrate the authenticity of the neighborhood. It was as if the Dominicans, Puerto Ricans, Cubans, and Salvadorians had allowed Columbia to enter the community with the understanding that the neighborhood was and would remain theirs. So despite walking into a classroom that had few black people, I knew that something about this was metaphorical. I didn't have to go searching for a way to infiltrate a neighborhood. I merely had to walk out the front door of the nursing school and get to work. I wanted to make a difference, and the school was perfectly placed for that.

Despite all the fear and pressure, I felt a peace and calm when I got to walk around the blocks of 168th Street and Broadway and ride the train. It's a feeling that those who have never been in a minority position cannot understand. There is a weight off your shoulders and a sense of peace that sits within when you enter a space with people of common experiences. The nursing school and medical campus were also home to a homeless shelter. This gave the area a different type of grit that wasn't present on the main campus. I don't think parents shipping their eighteen-year-old off to college would have the same appreciation I gained from having this reality so close. Yes, from time to time, there were altercations with beggars or the mentally ill. But that's what made the place so beautiful to me. You weren't free to ignore the truths of the world and the complexities therein.

Columbia set minimum qualifications for its admitted students, but within them was a sense of normalcy. Students didn't have to possess some special gene or "it" quality. Many of the applicants just had a desire to do more and to achieve to a higher degree to realize their own dreams. That made me appreciate the importance of just trying, or even more so, the importance of not hindering someone else's dreams. My cohorts were like a "who's who" of diversity: a Filipino woman, a black woman, a Taiwanese woman, a gay white man, and me. If anyone needed an example of what diversity looked like, we could've been the poster children.

We each had a desire to contribute to our community in a larger capacity and saw a doctorate in nursing practice as a way to achieve that. Having that common goal allowed us to embrace each other as we learned cultural and life experiences from one another. It felt safe as we interacted with one another in our small groups, and we also developed a certain dependency on one another for venting and accountability. There was no arrogance within our cohort; none of us came from blue blood or aristocratic backgrounds, and we each brought experiences to the conversation that allowed us to debate and collaborate in robust manners. Everyone had something to offer.

One of the great benefits of being part of the academic world is that resources are abundant, so there are opportunities to participate in groundbreaking research. I felt this directly as my cohort and other students worked our way through the classes and semesters and were expected to submit posters, abstracts, presentations, and manuscripts to conferences and peer-reviewed journals. The opportunity to be an active participant within the professional community was at my fingertips, and the faculty were glad to assist and support me along the way.

I had the thought in the back of my mind that I would like to be a published author, but I didn't think I would be forced to run head-on into the process. I found myself challenged in a new way to look beyond the audience of my classmates and professors to a regional, national, and even international audience. During my time at Columbia, I not only successfully submitted and published my first manuscript, but I also had the opportunity to be a presenter alongside a couple of my classmates when our poster projects were accepted by a regional conference. We were expected to be leaders within our specialty as well as take advantage of the opportunities within our professional conferences. My work was tangible. I was a voice for change, and a beacon of light for those behind me.

After I completed my program—and even during it—I was presented with various opportunities within my profession and academia. I didn't know exactly which path I desired to take after getting my doctorate, but I did know the degree would be an added qualification that could afford me an invitation into those previously closed-door meetings. There would be invitations for increased responsibility at my job, including to serve as a member on a hospital board or to lead a committee for initiatives within the hospital system. Most directly, there were new opportunities to teach or to be an adjunct or tenure-track professor at a university. There seemed to be an open basket of options available to me.

I can't say for sure that Columbia was the reason for my professional successes, but it was a major catalyst. I am not totally sold on the idea that my institution made me the quality candidate and professional I am today. I also value the great benefit of attending a less notable school, achieving the same degree and qualifications necessary to complete a terminal degree, and doing it all debt-free or at a much lower cost. The most important thing I got from Columbia was the ability to tell children and others within my community that anything is possible. I even witnessed a new interest, or superficial respect, from that same surgeon who questioned my shoe choice. After someone mentioned that I was pursuing my doctorate at Columbia, he suddenly became more interested in who I was as a person. I know that illusion of admiration too well. It solidified my notion that we need more people like me in academic arenas. I believe my presence and participation as a nontraditional doctoral student enriched Columbia's program and the experiences of those within it. My views, perspectives, and experiences provided insights into a world few in my program had experienced.

I graduated from Columbia in 2017. Since then, I've been able to leverage my passion and professional skills to be nominated to a board seat within the Diversity in Nurse Anesthesia Mentorship Program. The program has also allowed me to be the beacon I sought to be and to stand as an example for less-advantaged children and individuals pursuing a path to financial freedom and a fulfilling career beyond stereotypes. The effort to improve our communities is ongoing as I work to position myself as an approachable resource.

The importance of mentoring and the need for additional support within the construct and culture of education is evidenced by statistics showing that, despite their completion of nursing programs, males and minorities (Black, Hispanic, and Asian) consistently have lower pass rates than their white counterparts, according to retrospective studies analyzing the pass-fail results on NCLEX-RN test takers (Lima, M., London, L. and Manieri, E., 2011).

I want to encourage all of my fellow brothers and sisters who may have felt defeated, who may have not seen the examples or had access to the assets needed to inform and guide their educational and career decisions. I believe it's invaluable for youth to see themselves in others.

POSTSCRIPT

Today, after overcoming all the challenges and obstacles, I find myself in yet another fight. During the years and countless hours of studying, practicing, and striving to amass accolades, I found it easy to neglect my personal life. I viewed taking attention away from my professional goals as a distraction. I feared personal enjoyments would derail my career path. But in the strange turn of my professional fate, which was my decision to leave Atlanta and move to New York City, I also saw a turning point in my personal life.

Before I made the official move to New York, I had a Fourth of July celebration in Brooklyn on my itinerary. The party was atop my friend Julie's rooftop. That night still lives on as one of the most memorable and talked-about parties any of us have ever experienced. For me, it is even more memorable because at that party I met my future wife: Ashlee. Yes, the same Ashlee I was visiting the weekend I received the impromptu job interview and subsequent job offer.

Ashlee is brilliant and dynamically beautiful, and she's more refined version of myself. She's also from Tennessee—Memphis, to be exact—and how interesting it is that our paths crossed in New York. When we first met, I don't think she considered the potential, as I was still commuting back and forth from Atlanta during the moving transition. To her surprise, I was back and presenting some permanence just two months after we met.

As many who know me could attest, it's never been easy for me to stand still and allow others to get close to me. But Ashlee has been the stability I've needed to ground myself in this new stage of life. She's been integral in helping me express myself both inside and out while also providing me the support I need to heal old wounds. Her personality as an inherent nurturer coupled with her PhD in psychology have made her a driving force for my maturation as a partner.

Five years after moving to New York, my focus has turned toward learning how to balance life. Today, we live in New Orleans. We moved when Ashlee began her PhD program at Tulane University. My professional ambitions have pivoted to mentoring and encouraging young adults and people of color. My goal is to educate and inform others of the same tools and opportunities that have provided families financial security for numerous decades.

I'm learning to pour as much into my home and family as I pour into students and patients. With Ashlee as co-captain, I understand that sacrificing and compromising for the mutual growth of the whole are key. Together, hand-in-hand, the road continues to rise to meet us as we "Dream Big" together!

ABOUT THE AUTHOR

'Doc Flanagan' loves to learn and to achieve, as his credentials attest. He has earned a Doctorate of Nursing Practice from Columbia University, a Master of Science of Nursing from Samford University, and a Bachelor of Science of Nursing from Emory University. He now practices in New Orleans. His biggest passion—outside of his work and his wife—is helping those interested in nursing. He knows from sometimes painful experiences that, "You can't be what you don't see." (That's Doc's other mantra.) So he's set up the Dream Big Mentorship Program to offer support, guidance, and wealth-building strategies to nurse anesthesia school candidates, particularly non-traditional ones. He travels the country to spread the word. To find out more, go to www.drdonteflanagan.com

Made in the USA
Columbia, SC
14 August 2020

076